WHAT OTHERS ARE SAYING

"I first met Ted "Rock" Knapp in 2008 on a recruiting trip to Albany Georgia to check out one of his players. He had only just weeks before been given his grim prognosis. You never would have known it and in fact it wasn't until some time later that I actually believed it. The coach that I was meeting for the first time was living life to the fullest. The same passion, enthusiasm and confidence that he overwhelmed me with that day jumps off the pages of Bury Me with My Whistle. If you want to laugh a little, cry a little and think a lot; this is the book for you. Funny thing is, the young man I went to see, we decided to pass on him. Yet it was still one of the most productive recruiting trips of my career because of the relationship that was forged with Rock. I know you will feel the same way after reading this book. The Good Lord sure works in strange ways."

—Charlie Skalaski
College and NFL Assistant Coach
Currently Director of Player Personnel at Liberty University

"Ted is a great football coach (in three seasons playing for him my sons did not lose a single game). However, his real gift is for mentoring, coaching and building the character of young men. Again, never underestimate the impact of a strong Christian man in the life of a young boy."

—Phil Kershaw, Former Chairman, Canadian Football League.

"Outside of my dad, my high school wrestling coach was the most influential man in my life growing up. Coach Knapp's book reminded me of that and of the significant role a coach plays in a young athlete's life. But the truth is, the lessons he shares here aren't just for athletes. They can truly inspire us all."

—Dan Cathy
Chairman, President and CEO of Chick-fil-A

"This book is a must read for anyone who loves the game of football. I know something about winner's as I was the Special Teams Captain of the 1972 undefeated Superbowl Champion Miami Dolphins. I worked as an assistant under Coach Knapp for two years going unbeaten in both campaigns. He is a master motivator, life-changing mentor and example of everything a Christian coach should be. This book is a must read for anyone who loves the Lord!"

—Lloyd Mumphord
Special Teams Captain
1972 Superbowl Miami Dolphins

"It is rare for one book to tackle so many subjects with such depth and passion. The stories are riveting, the relationships will move you to deep emotion and the spiritual life of this man and his family will inspire all."

—Art Briles
Head Football Coach
Baylor University

Wow, what a read! I could not put it down. A coaching Bible for the young coach, the veteran coach, male coaches, female coaches, every parent, school administrators and fans of every sport. To his credit, Knapp does not leave his cancer or faith in some private recess of his mind or book. He has no fear of dying and his trust in God is unshakeable.

—Chuch Faucette
Former NFL Linebacker
Head Football Coach
Lutheran South High
St. Louis, Missouri

BURY ME WITH MY WHISTLE

TED "ROCK" KNAPP

BURY ME WITH MY WHISTLE

TATE PUBLISHING
AND ENTERPRISES, LLC

Bury Me With My Whistle
Copyright © 2014 by Ted "Rock" Knapp. All rights reserved.

No part of this publication may be reproduced, stored in a retrieval system or transmitted in any way by any means, electronic, mechanical, photocopy, recording or otherwise without the prior permission of the author except as provided by USA copyright law.

The opinions expressed by the author are not necessarily those of Tate Publishing, LLC.

Published by Tate Publishing & Enterprises, LLC
127 E. Trade Center Terrace | Mustang, Oklahoma 73064 USA
1.888.361.9473 | www.tatepublishing.com

Tate Publishing is committed to excellence in the publishing industry. The company reflects the philosophy established by the founders, based on Psalm 68:11,
"The Lord gave the word and great was the company of those who published it."

Book design copyright © 2014 by Tate Publishing, LLC. All rights reserved.
Cover design by Gian Philipp Rufin
Interior design by Manolito Bastasa

Published in the United States of America

ISBN: 978-1-63306-023-4
Sports & Recreation / Football
14.07.10

DEDICATION

There were many deserving family members and friends to whom I could have dedicated this book. One stood out and made my decision an easy choice. Mark Tidwell wrote an entire chapter at the beginning of this book, and you'll have no problem recognizing a man of great faith and character. He fought colon cancer for five years before finally going home. Mark led my very first high school football team to the Georgia state title as my quarterback and captain. Mark chose coaching as his profession, and in those years, he burned it up as part of eight state titles in several sports. These last many years, he became an area director for FCA on the north side of Atlanta. His ministry has touched hundreds and hundreds for the Lord. He had his own ministry called, Leave a Mark, which he writes about in his chapter, "Leave a Mark."

Mark passed away on March 21, 2014; he had just turned fifty years old. He leaves behind his wife, Lee, of twenty-eight years. Together, they had three children: Nathan, married to Kristen, parents of Camden Grace; Jessica, married to Dennis Coyle; and Cameron, married to Caitlin. Parents, Bob and Patty Tidwell, live in Orange Beach, Alabama. I've seen Mark numerous times through the years since he was my signal caller in 1980. Each time our paths crossed, he was gaining greater influence, speaking to the Falcons on game day, and who could forget, just weeks before passing away and just after major surgery, he spoke to the

Kell football team and twenty-five boys gave their lives to Jesus Christ! That, my friends, is leaving a mark!

I will live out the rest of my days remembering Mark as his football and basketball coach and, in the end, his friend and brother. I'll never claim a higher honor. It is my great pleasure to dedicate this book in his memory.

ACKNOWLEDGMENT

I would like to thank Janie Neighbors for her time and effort as my initial proofreader. I've never had a better partner in my thirty years in Christian education. She is one of a kind. I would like to thank Phil Kershaw for his valuable contribution as a consultant and advisor on this project. I would like to thank Delta Dave Tribo. His support, encouragement, and technical direction and editing got me over the hump and into the Library of Congress! I am indebted forever to "the boys" who in days gone by answered to the call of my whistle; nine state titles, playing for five others and memories of one great ride deserving the attention of Grantland Rice. Last but not least, this book would never have happened without the daily love, care, and patient counsel of my wonderful wife, Shari.

CONTENTS

Foreword 15
Preface 19
Gridiron Guru 21
For All Young Guns 27
Conflict Management 83
Pigskin Playbook 95
Rock Reflects 117
Devotionals 127
Gridiron Gossip and Graffiti 207
About the Author 219

FOREWORD

I was headmaster at a Christian school where our football coach had suddenly quit after taking another job late in the school year. The team had gone 0-10 the previous fall and, over the years, was a team everyone wanted as their homecoming opponent. Spring practice was about to begin, and prospects for a new head football coach that late in the year were thin. I do not recall how Rock had heard about the opening, but I do remember getting a thick package with page after page of remarkable coaching accomplishments. It was one of those "too good to be true" moments followed by "why would he want to come to our school?"

It was in late spring of 1995 in a Cajun restaurant along a freeway in North Houston that I first met Rock and Shari Knapp. I do not recall talking about Xs and Os (which would have been wasted on me anyway, having been encouraged by my high school football coach to go out for cross-country since he had me run so much as the team clown), but I do remember talking about our faith, Jesus Christ, and the remarkable opportunities football provided to build boys into godly men. There was an immediate connection, and when I asked when he could start, I fully expected him to pull out his whistle and rush over to school for spring practice. He did make it to spring practice and rallied the few boys left on the team to set aside their personal agendas and commit to an agenda of all-out training and conditioning that would continue through the summer up to the opening day of football. Rock would go on to build a program to be perennial play-off contenders and state champions. The package that I had received that spring was true; Rock built boys into godly men who also found success on the football field.

Since prehistoric times, artists have sought to set free the images that they see trapped within rock. The methods they use have evolved over the centuries, but the basic process stays the same: the artist must remove the unnecessary material. It is a process of elimination. Michelangelo is quoted as saying, "In every block of marble I see a statue as plain as though it stood before me, shaped and perfect in attitude and action. I have only to hew away the rough walls that imprison the lovely apparition to reveal it to the other eyes as mine see it." That is how God sees us. Just as the artist can see the art inside the block of stone, God can see the potential inside of us. There are cracks that are sometimes well hidden. But God can work wonders with the material he created. God uses people, circumstances, and yes, football coaches, and even cancer, to fill in the flaws and chip away, eliminate our ungodliness, for our good and his purpose.

So rather than a football book for coaches with intricate plays (Xs and Os) and training schedules, this is a book about sculpting. How one man, a player and coach, has been formed by football, and now terminal cancer, and how he has been used by God to use football to form godly men from boys. Through personal stories, Coach shares his struggles and triumphs, but most of all his uncommon, immeasurable love and relationship with Jesus Christ. His boys, now men, share their testimonies of how Coach's uncompromising dedication and zeal for excellence and his love for them and Jesus Christ changed their lives, not just on the football field, but for eternity. His family members share their stories, telling that in spite of his laser focus and love for football, he loved them well.

At the end of the game called life, remembering that we are terminal, a mark of man will not be measured how he turned out, but rather how those around him turned out. Coach has done it well as testified by countless former players and his family. Coach always led by example. In this book, he shares examples of how do it right and examples of what to avoid in the hope that the reader will impact the world for Jesus Christ through the game of football. He provides devotionals to build the biblical foundation, and ultimately, he gives praise and credit to Jesus Christ for any success he can claim.

Every coach and player is like a block of stone, there's greatness inside, but it has to be carved out. It has to be carved out through hard work, dedication, blood, sweat, and tears; it has to be carved out by an individual who can perceive their own greatness as seen by God as well as greatness in others. I know it is Coach's prayer that this book will play an important part in the sculpting process for coaches and players alike.

In his grip,

Glenn Holzman, PhD
March 22, 2014
Micah 6:8

PREFACE

Looking for a good read, huh? I feel pretty good about this one. One thing for sure, you won't find another book like it anywhere in the entire Library of Congress. The fact that I'm terminally ill with two fatal diseases automatically narrows the field in terms of a rare and unique read. Secondly, I'm a storyteller. Stories seem to have a longer shelf life than simple facts or even organized information. And people love a good story. I so hope this "pigskin project" inspires you to dream big and maybe even tackle life with a little more passion. Above all other motives, I am writing this book to share my first-person adventures of the awesome companionship of my Redeemer and Lord through my thirty-year career as a head football coach and, especially these last six years, as Christ has been my all in all.

The book morphs from one genre to another, but there are two constants you can expect throughout its pages: football and spiritual perspective. Not only are there dozens of stories reminiscent of Friday nights under the lights—there is an entire season worth of devotionals for coaches. You will also find a hybrid playbook of my organizational checklist, my team rules and expectations, my philosophy of winning, my approach to motivation, and my great passion for building a love for one another that lasts a lifetime. I share coaching dos and don'ts with young coaches using actual letters written by former players that will pack quite a punch. The last chapter of the book is an intimate look into our personal journey these past six years of battling terminal cancer. My wife contributes her perspective, and together, we want to bring hope to all those fighting to survive.

    I have lived a full life. My wife of thirty-four years, my five children, and my nine grandbabies make me the most blessed man on the planet. Each day in which I'm still vertical and able to smell the morning coffee is a day of good reasons for celebration! My thirty years of being allowed to have such incredible access to the hearts of thousands of teenagers has been the rarest of privileges and the most satisfying and exciting vocation on earth. Each new day brought the potential for miracles and the chance to give unconditional love and change lives, all the while doing so with a whistle around my neck and Christ in my heart. And soon enough, I will see him face-to-face and will exchange my whistle for a victor's crown! So please don't forget, bury me with my whistle.

GRIDIRON GURU

I am not your normal football fan. My obsession began as a four-year-old. I could rattle off all the teams of the Big Ten Conference before I could cite the twelve months of the year. I talked my dad into letting me play that fall season! I can remember standing in front of the mirror in my parent's bedroom in my very first game uniform (red jersey and white pants of the Kankakee Moose), staring at myself, mouthpiece in and helmet buckled. I remember at such a young age, sitting down on the edge of their bed and crying because I wanted to take that red uniform off and emerge back in front of the mirror in the magical black and gold of the Iowa Hawkeyes! I was four and ready for the Big Ten! I did not understand why I couldn't just be a Hawkeye my first season. I could be taking handoffs from Hawkeye quarterback Ed Podolak and making pudding out of Purdue or galloping through those loafers known as Gophers! Apparently, eventually, Dad talked me into believing that the Hawkeyes would keep a opening on the roster while I helped bring home the county championship to the mighty, mighty Moose.

Why Iowa? We were Iowa people. I was born in Des Moines, and both my parents spent their younger days living in the eastern part of the state. Dad and I would sit for hours listening to radio station WHO Des Moines and Hawkeye games on Saturday afternoons in his station wagon. We lived in Kankakee, Illinois (less than an hour south of the loop), which happened to be well within the strong Midwest radio signal of WHO Des Moines. We listened to the pregame and postgame shows. We cheered loud and proud, and our neighbors always got a kick out of our Saturday father-son ritual. Heck, for fourteen years, I got the honor of laying on the horn anytime Iowa scored! Needless to say, it was rare enough that I was never in danger of waking up our neighbors from their Saturday afternoon naps. Although the Hawks went almost two decades without a winning season, it did not matter to this young boy. I was with my dad. He talked to me, he drove us through the A&W Root Beer drive-in or the Dairy Queen (always at halftime), and he taught me things about the game I would never forget even to this day over a half century later. There was nothing like the game of football. There was no team like Iowa. And there was no man on earth to compare to my dad, if not but for a few short hours on the fall weekends of my childhood.

Football has always been the passion of my life. Little did I know that as I reached my college years that I could actually be paid for my lifelong addiction! This game of the gridiron would become the catalyst and channel by which I would launch thousands of meaningful relationships, and that the game of football would cast me into a lifelong identity as coach. So bury me in a suit and tie? Doesn't seem quite right to this old crusty linebacker. So I'd sure appreciate it if my first whistle from my first team and first state title from the 1980 season would be positioned around my neck. I'd like my oldest son to do the honors. He continues the legacy of Coach Knapp—you might want to hold on to your first whistle too, son. Just sayin'.

If I may, let's talk more football and hark back to the roads travelled to eventually arrive at my calling as a football coach. Let me begin by clearly stating one very important detail that weighed heavy in terms of my journey and transformation into a gridiron guru. That detail is very obvious; I played eighteen straight years of football, all in pads, no flags, and no soccer balls. I played ten years in the peewee leagues, four years of high school ball, and finished with four stellar years at the collegiate level. Do anything for eighteen years, and you'll develop instincts that ripen into skill mastery and catapult you into the rare air where only eagles fly. I never had to watch much film in *college in order to line up at linebacker and pick up little signals telling me exactly where the ball was going. My coach knew this and let me line up wherever I wanted just before the snap of the ball. I was on my own to stunt, drop into coverage, or simply hold my ground. I averaged twenty-four tackles a game my junior year. I was nearly unstoppable because of my football ESP. There were three games my junior year that at the end of the game, the opposing head coach shook my hand and told me that I had just played the greatest game of football they had ever seen. In fact, the coach who replaced my college coach actually called me one night at home about fifteen years after my career ended to ask me if the stats kept by Dr. Weeks (college VP) were true. He didn't believe the numbers he was reading in regard to my season by season tackle totals. Oh, what I would give for one more mad dash from the blindside with my target in sight and the roar of the crowd.*

When you do the math, I have spent forty-eight of my fifty-seven years either wearing a helmet on my head or a whistle around my neck. I'm a football man. I am most happy on the sidelines. A distant second is a deer stand, and off-shore fishing comes in a close third. Only recently have I found another hobby, which provides a real challenge and plenty of enjoyment—authoring books! But regardless of how many deer I mount on the wall or record number of fish I catch or best-sellers I write, football is king of the Knapp clan. My middle name is Mojo, and just for the record, thirty straight years having never deferred to the second half. Never the hunted, always the hunter!

People often refer to me as a gridiron savant and believe I have some magical aptitude for the science of blocking and tackling. Well, I'm no savant and I carry no magic dust. I simply submit to you that when anyone spends a half century engrossed in one enterprise, they automatically develop certain instincts and insights reserved for those of us "married" to our lifelong craft. Nine state titles, as well as playing in five other championship games, is a result of one simple Bible axiom, "You reap what you sow," or as I have said ten million times, "Input equals output!" We'll win because we'll outwork the rest of the world!

I've been a very blessed man to have been chosen for this incredible journey, and as you will see, a journey full of overcoming the impossible, of heart-stopping drama, a journey that chronicles the immeasurable love between one coach and his boys. The best part of it all is the way our common bond of football has drawn us to an uncommon, immeasurable love and relationship with Jesus Christ. Yes, football has been that facilitator. This pigskin project hopes to use the sport of gladiators to inspire you to dream big, maybe tackle life with a little more passion, and I would ask you to consider all the wonderful works of Christ in my life along the way, leading to this very moment. I declare him irresistible.

Another very important aspect of the game of football is love. Yes, love. I am often asked by other coaches about the secret to all my success. They begin to interrogate my offensive or defensive philosophies; they want to gain insight into our organization and preparation in terms of player development and strategies to gain advantage over our opponents. Well, let's be honest. Put one hundred coaches in a room together, and it won't take long to realize they all have their own leadership style and belief system as to what works best on both sides of the line of scrimmage, and under real scrutiny, you'll discover we all are copycats to one degree or another. I'll confess to the latter. I've always tried to be innovative, and I think I did a good job of preparing my teams. However, it was never about outsmarting the other guy; it was much more about outworking him. But the real key ingredient to championship football is love. I loved my players with a fierce love, an unconditional love, and a willingness to help them dream big dreams. The result? They loved me back with the same love and loyalty. To this day, I have a love affair with hundreds and hundreds of former players that neither time nor distance can ever weaken. And when you need your players to run through a wall or take an enemy hill, they will leave nothing, having given the full measure of the man, his blood, sweat, tears, and heart.

I recently was turning the channel on our TV when I settled on Imus in the Morning. He was interviewing former Senator Tom

Bradley of New York. Imus pointed out that the Knicks had not won a championship since Bradley won two for New York way back in the day. (Bradley also won a gold medal in the '64 Olympics.) Imus asked the Hall of Famer what he thought was the right formula for winning a championship. I loved Bradley's answer. He said you go out and draft character first, rather than statistics. Go get a group of men who will put the team first and their individual egos in a safety deposit box somewhere. He said today, everyone wants to be the star. He illustrated the team first concept by explaining that a star has five points and that each player must take his place as one of the points rather than the whole star. Once you have each of your main characters fulfilling his role, then within a short period of time, they will begin to love each other as a result of their common bond. Once love and trust abounds, you can set your sights on world champions!

So this game of football, as you will see through the storytelling of many, simulates war like no other sport known to man. It develops courage, leadership, mental toughness, selflessness, discipline, and even good manners. But the greatest of these, the game changer, is love. Here now is a limited player's collection of a half century of love, laughter, and life lessons.

FOR ALL YOUNG GUNS

My hope is as you read these selected letters and e-mails, you will see yourself in the years ahead. There is a world of young people just waiting for someone to believe in them, to build them up, help them dream big dreams, and mentor them in the things that matter most. No one is better positioned to be that lifelong hero than you—the coach! Don't bully or browbeat, never stoop to name-calling, and know the difference between motivation and manipulation. Make the game fun; never treat the kids all the same, either. They're not the same. Each athlete has their own specific needs and will respond with great enthusiasm to a coach who shows constant love and interest in the person first, player second. Be an example and an influence with your own behavior demonstrating strong leadership, character, discipline, honesty, and selflessness. Be able to laugh at yourself and be approachable at all times—being moody will poison the entire team atmosphere. Let every decision be driven by one thing; is it in the best interest of the boys (or girls)?

You do the things I just mentioned, and you can expect the same lifelong relationships I am sharing with you in these letters. These excerpts are just a few of hundreds and hundreds of letters, e-mails, cards, phone calls, and home visits, especially these past five years. I am a man most blessed; in fact, I think of myself as the most blessed man alive. You could be next.

First up, my first quarterback, first MVP, first captain, first to lead a team to the state title! He will be the first story to leave a mark.

Winning Words
by Mark Tidwell
Philippians 3:13–14

I wasn't used to failing. In fact, rarely had I ever felt like a failure up to that point in my life. But that late fall night, as a sixteen-year-old junior, seated around a bunch of my high school teammates, I felt it. What's worse, I was the supposed leader. I was the quarterback of an overachieving young football squad who had clawed its way into the state championship game at the end of its inaugural season. We had defied the odds most of the year and had come away victorious in nearly every game, but here we were at halftime of the biggest one of the year, and we looked like whipped pups as we nursed a 0-14 deficit. I had orchestrated an offense, which had churned out -8 yards total. That's *minus* 8 yards. There was no one to blame, in my mind, but myself, and *I was failing*...miserably.

Most of the heads in that locker room were down and most eyes on the floor. Danny Sweatmon, an incredibly talented tailback (6'3", 190 lbs) and an emotional player, was pacing and mumbling to himself and others. But mostly, we sat shocked, feeling the pain, as the first half thrashing became a reality. Our coach, Ted Knapp, was being interviewed by the local radio station, so we were left to ourselves to come up with some pretty quick answers, if we were to save face at all in the second half. A couple of us began to speak and share our feelings and then Coach Knapp came in. His halftime speech and adjustments were as close to Knute Rockne as any I've ever witnessed! We looked at each other around the now standing circle of warriors, and we began to feel it. We saw hope, we felt renewed energy, a spirit flowed through the room that only athletes can feel at moments like that. The resolve to reenter the arena of battle took root, and we bolted out of the tunnel to take the field.

Between my former teammates and me, we could probably piece together the exact plays and order of events of the next twenty minutes that ticked off the game clock. There was an interception by our noseguard who returned the ball for a touchdown, there were a couple of incredible catches by our sure-handed freshman receiver, our sophomore running back/safety showed speed that took the other team by surprise, both sides of our line began manhandling the other side, our junior tailback was as good as he had ever been, and our senior fullback/linebacker played like a man possessed. I don't even remember what all I did; there were some passes completed and some decent runs, but I had never played in a contest in which an entire collection of boys played that way as a team. When the dust cleared, we had blanked the opposing team and had scored at will. The final score showed 30-14…*us!*

Failure and success. Both were felt on that night back in 1980. At least, by the definitions our culture of sport, and society in general, would place upon those events. But since that amazing state championship win (Georgia Peachstate League), life has proven to be a wise teacher. I will admit, it has taken a long while for me to grasp many of its lessons, especially in regard to winning and losing, success and failure. During that school year, I decided my life career goal was to be a coach; much of that desire came after the influence Coach Knapp had on me and the effect I saw possible on high school students. I went on to be a high school coach and, twenty years later, had the privilege of claiming eight state titles in five different sports (baseball, basketball, football, girls' softball, and track/field).

Today, those rings sit in my drawer every day, the ones I still have. Rarely does one emerge to be worn for a special occasion. Time has a way of dulling the luster of significance we place on certain accomplishments. You see, I am facing a different battle now, and the wins and seeming losses have taken on a different definition. The field has been replaced by hospitals and operating rooms; my coaches are now my doctors and nurses; workouts substituted by medical treatments, therapies, drugs, supplements, and specific nutrients; my teammates are my wife, kids, parents, siblings, and families, relatives, and friends, and other victims. Victims whose opponent is cancer. Every day now, not just Friday nights, I compete. For over four years, this dreaded disease and I have squared off each and every morning, and many long, restless nights. Six times, I have been told, "You lost," that cancer had showed up and/or returned. In the first three years, the surgeons cut me open and did battle. Each time left another scar, but I was able to suit up again, just moving a little slower each time. When the experts from the best medical facilities in the country (MD Anderson, Vanderbilt, Mayo Clinic, etc.) announced to us "stage 4," the statistics indeed said that we were in the fourth quarter with the clock ticking.

But another coach has been recruited and he has the game plan. He has revealed that he is not finished with me yet, and that I am not going to be pulled from the game just yet. His script and strategy are not traditional and do not necessarily follow the norm. I feel I am to be following a set of plays that was revealed by him three years into this journey. In the summer of 2012, we began a project and campaign called Leave a Mark. In fact, I was inspired to use this phrase after seeing a caption on a football t-shirt, under a crushing tackle, which read, "Ooh, that's gonna leave a mark!" In October of the same year, I published my first book by the same name, *Leave a Mark*.

My passion and desire is to "inspire and motivate individuals to fulfill the purpose for which they were created." Because I now see every day as so very precious, my focus has been redirected and I treasure each even more. With each day come more opportunities to touch those lives around whom we've been placed.

I want to not only do my part, but to encourage others to do the same. What talents and tools have you been given? Are they being used to serve others and to make a mark on this world? We have incredible possibilities to *impact* and *influence* those around us, but are we being *intentional* about it? Those three words can change our game plan. If we would but be aware of these opportunities, we would leave a mark and impress upon others values and truths that would make a difference in their lives.

Bottom line: I am terminal, but we *all* are. We have a set number of days on this earth, of which no one knows but our Creator. He has a path for us, and we are to seek what that path and plan are (Jeremiah 29:11–13). As Coach Knapp did, and so many coaches and players do across our world, we have to have a game plan to be successful. Without one, we will most assuredly fail. But the same falls true in life. What is your plan? If you are not at peace about this life and especially life beyond in eternity, that game plan is vital. You need to have the Coach as your Lord. This involves a personal relationship with him, not just a blind acknowledgment of his presence. If you do have peace about that aspect, then the question for you (and all of us) is "What now?" What are we doing each and every day to fulfill that purpose, that game plan?

Failure, success. Lots of definitions and thoughts surround these terms. Be sure your definitions align with God's and that your game plan is one which comes from his playbook.

Mark has a Web site with his story and more info at www.leaveamarknow.com. His book, shirts, jewelry, and wristbands can be ordered there. Be sure to watch the short video with his inspirational message.

Holy Lou Holtz!

> The Sovereign Lord is my strength; He makes my feet like the feet of a deer, He enables me to go on the heights!
>
> Habakkuk 3:19 KJV

Let's talk tubas and the marching band. It was a Saturday morning, and as was always the case, the football team gathered together to play a couple of hours of fiercely contested basketball. It accomplished a couple of deliberate purposes. First, it was part of our weekly conditioning. Although we lifted weights and ran all five days of the week, we liked the idea of making Saturday our Lagniappe (appropriate Cajun word meaning "icing on the cake!"), conditioning advantage over opponents who slept in on Saturday or lay around watching *Scooby Doo* or *Pee Wee's Playhouse*. Secondly, because we were a private school (Westminster Christian Academy), we had to actively recruit student athletes, and we used our Saturday pick-up games for our players to invite their friends to come play and maybe we could connect in such a way as to cause them to take interest in our school and program. Well, I never knew what was going to walk through the gym lobby and out onto the court. And I remember one particular Saturday more than any other.

Reggie Richard was one of our recruits. Reggie had a great career as a Crusader and had a very unique story of his own. You see, Reg was only 5'6" and 155 pounds. Believe it or not, he played right guard on offense. This is a team that had back-to-back undefeated seasons. We were good. Reggie was one of the reasons for our success. He was small, but he was so aggressive and so stinkin' quick that he could get into a defender's legs and open holes on a consistent basis. He played on every one of our special teams and was always, without exception, the first guy downfield to make a play. Leslie Frazier, at the time the head football coach for Trinity International in Chicago (NAIA), offered this undeniably undersized player a scholarship to play at Trinity. Coach Frazier said Reggie would be one of the best special team's players in the country because of his incredible effort and resolve to make every play. Leslie Frazier is presently the head coach of the Minnesota Vikings.

It was early April, and Reggie had brought his cousin to the Saturday pick-up game. His cousin was a good-looking specimen. His name was Shelton Jordan, and he was all of 6'4" and 205 lbs. I asked him if he played football at his present public school, and he made it clear he played basketball, but the rest of the year, he was the tuba player in the marching band. I wrote him off as a prospect upon hearing his love for the tuba. Immediately following that conversation, we started running the court and playing basketball (or what some might call WWF). It did not take but a minute or so for me to watch Shelton go up for a rebound high enough for me to see the bottom of his shoes! He could run like the wind, jump out of the gym, and was immovable in the paint. He was as articulate and polite as he was a prototype big-time college rush end. After several weeks of inviting him to church and attempting to meet with his parents, it finally all came together and we got one heck of a tuba player on the roster. Shelton had never played football. He was quite raw and had a big learning curve in front of him. No worries, he played his first game of the '93 season at 6'4", 255 lbs. He was ripped and scary looking from the left offensive tackle's viewpoint. By the time he played his last game of his senior season, he had leveled out at 6'5" and a whopping 280 lbs.! He went into the national recruiting season ranked as the number 2 defensive player in the nation. In the end, he decided to accept a full football scholarship to the University of Notre Dame. Lou Holtz flew in, ate Mama's cookin', and hugged all our necks and said, "I love you." Go Irish.

We all learned a great truth from Shelton. Within each of us is great potential and the ability to accomplish the biggest of dreams. We simply must be willing to risk sailing our vessel out into the deep waters rather than sitting upon the shoreline, satisfied. Keep in mind that if we are walking with our Savior in obedience to his Word, then he will give us the desires of our hearts! So go ahead and run like a deer and dare to take the mountain. God has put great potential in you and a plan of success beyond your wildest dreams.

Climbing the Mountain of Mental Toughness
by Chris Harrell
James 1:12

When I was a junior in high school in the fall of 1987, I played football for Coach Knapp. Coach was a gentleman, but on the football field, he often admonished us to play with a killer instinct. One afternoon, he grew weary of the lack of intensity our team was displaying in blocking and tackling. In his frustration, he halted practice and called the entire team together. We formed ourselves into a circle while Coach stood there with a tight-mouthed expression on his face.

When we all arrived, Coach explained that he was not happy with the level of effort we were putting into practice. His words were nothing extraordinary, but the tension in his voice and sharp and abrupt gestures he used as he dressed us down conveyed that we were failing to do something important. Coach said that we were running the plays correctly and fast enough, but that we were just going through the motions. That we were not really hitting each other.

As a 165 lbs. nearsighted tackling dummy, the player I most respected, and at times feared, was Jason Burns. Jason was our best defensive linebacker. We were both about six feet tall, but Jason weighed about 235 lbs. and had a real mean streak. Earlier that season, Jason had broken an opponent's sternum as the player attempted to run through a hole, and Jason met him head on (footnote 1). We watched in awe from the sidelines as the game stopped, and the opponent was carried off the field on a stretcher. I knew how that guy felt, and when we were running drills, I did all I could to avoid any position that would put me in front of Jason.

What surprised me most about what Coach was saying was the puzzled expression on Jason's face. Jason was the person I most expected to understand hitting hard, with a killer instinct, and it was becoming evident to me that there was a significant gap between Coach Knapp's understanding of the quality of our practice and Jason's. As I watched the question forming on Jason's face, knowing it would likely just increase Coach's angst, I stood there watching, caught up in the current of what was happening, knowing that when the wave of Coach's wrath broke, it would wash over all of us, and we would pay for not listening and understanding with greater sweat and exhaustion.

But something else happened. Jason asked his question, and I watch something resolve in Coach's mind. He dropped his clipboard on the ground, spread his feet apart slightly, brought his arms up in front of him, and told Jason to hit him as hard as he could and to not hold anything back. He added that Jason was not going to hurt him.

I could see from Jason's face that while the thought of hurting Coach had briefly troubled him, two impulses had won out in his mind. Jason was relishing the idea of payback for the particularly grueling regimen Coach had put us through that day, but more so, Jason was after all, a teenage boy, and at his core, he wanted to knock the old man off his feet so the young gun could stand in his place. While Jason wouldn't of course become coach, it would definitely register in Jason's mind and in the minds of everyone present who was the meanest wolf in the pack. After a brief pause, Jason chuckled as he confidently took a step back, crouched down, and charged.

My jaw dropped as I watched Jason gather speed toward Coach Knapp, and Coach just stood there. I knew Coach had played ball and felt confident he could handle himself, but Coach wasn't wearing protective gear, hadn't been practicing, and plus, he had to be thirty-five! And Jason was a monster, and now, he was charging at Coach as fast as he could, helmet down, his full weight behind him, and was now sailing through the air as Coach dropped his hips, brought his elbows in tight, and with a short, powerful movement, Coach hit Jason and sent him sprawling onto his back. Jason literally looked like an airborne cartoon character. He staggered through the rest of practice, trying to shake the cobwebs loose.

"Boys! That is what you are missing! That is what I have been telling you! You have to hit them like you mean it." Coach ended practice and turned us over to Coach Mitchell, who put us through his normal sadistic routine of torture euphemized as conditioning work.

That year of football, I learned an important lesson that I carried with me to the Naval Academy, into the Marines, and into many other situations in life. While I could have perhaps learned it in other settings, that particular football field, in that time and place, with those people, left a unique mark on me. I gained the kind of valuable knowledge that is combined with physical experience, and that only comes from enduring and suffering through something that is difficult. You see, I had no reason to be angry. I am not a worrier. I came from a stable and happy family. The only pressure I had ever felt came from my peers or from pressure that I put on myself. And while I knew how to work hard and my dad had taught me the importance of not giving up, I wasn't really mentally tough. I had no killer instinct and didn't really want one. But there are times in life when you have to fight the good fight, when you have to put it all on the line, and go after something with everything you have. Times when you risk injury, ruin, or death even, because there are people and things in life that are worth assuming that kind of risk. The mental process of deciding to go to war was not something I had then and therefore could not tap into. That day, when Coach Knapp disregarded his lack of conditioning, his age, the risk to his reputation, and potential physical injury to himself and decided in an instant to depend only on his mental resolve and struck down Jason Burns was the beginning of that lesson for me. I was on the football team because I showed up to all the practices and didn't quit and could hold a tackling dummy. I had the reputation of a pushover, and I rode the bench most games. But starting with Coach's display of deadly force, added with the prodding of my teammates, I began the process of letting go. One afternoon shortly afterward, I started hitting for real. I was never a starter, never a good football player, even. But I made the connection, heard the other player's equipment pop, and I earned the respect of the other players and, more importantly, my own self-respect.

I drew on that lesson when I stepped into the boxing ring at the Naval Academy. And each time I picked up a pugil stick at the Basic School as a marine lieutenant. And the first time I jumped out of an airplane, and at the times when I stepped off the helicopter into a place where people were shooting, and it's still there today for me to draw on whenever I need it, whether to do something myself, or to try to teach the lesson to my son or to a kid that I coach. People play sports for a lot of different reasons, but that year, I grabbed the brass ring and took it with me when I left. I wasn't in the starting lineup, and I didn't date a cheerleader, and I didn't get a football scholarship. But what I did get is more valuable than all those things combined. I got courage and guts. Do you have what it takes to conquer the world for Christ?

Rings and Wings
Rom. 8:38–39

This will be the most difficult selection of the book for me to write. My heart is so heavy, I find it somewhat hard to draw in a deep breath. You see, there comes along in every coach's life, one player who steals your heart above all others; for me, it was Brooks Bellow. You can see him in the picture section of the book, having just received his championship ring. He looks much more like a middle school manager than a varsity teammate. I'd guess Brooks at 5'6" and 140 lbs. soaking wet in pads and holding a 10 lb. bag of crawfish! But let the whole world know I never coached another player with his desire and heart. For two seasons, this runt of the litter started every varsity game and helped us claim back-to-back undefeated championships. Actually, had two guys at Westminster that found starting jobs just because of desire and courage, the other teammate was Jeremy Edwards, great kids!

Brooks loved football more than anything else in life. He was a man after my own heart. The sky would have fallen if I'd have ever had to criticize his effort. If you can imagine the great passion he demonstrated for our game going two full years on the field and in the weight room always being number 1 in effort, hustle, and attitude. If I were ever asked to build the perfect football player, the Warrior Wonder of Westminster, Brooks Bellow would be the blueprint (for which I would change nothing).

Brooks loved his coach. I could walk in the basketball arena where there might be 1,200 of our fans packed in the bleachers awaiting tip-off, and above the fray, I could feel Brooks's eyes following my every move. I've never seen a young man that was willing to completely surrender himself under the authority of his coach, not like Brooks. And don't think I didn't challenge him often. When you're no bigger than a minute and in order to compete and win his one-on-one's almost required he play in a total frenzy, never giving any forethought to bodily harm, he saw going against our 280 pounders as an opportunity to show us all he belonged out under those Friday night lights.

Several years ago now, we lost Brooks. It was a rainy day in Cajun country, and Brooks lost control of his car while taking a curve he had navigated a thousand times before. I was unable to make his funeral. I suppose not getting to go was the single most disappointing day of my coaching life. Brooks was buried with his game jersey on. When word came that he was buried in his jersey, well, I sobbed.

Will you help me honor this football man today? Here are the qualities that Brooks demonstrated every day, character qualities that made him a great lineman (often playing across the LOS against opponents who were literally a foot taller and 150 heavier!).

- Always on time
- Consistently great effort
- Very coachable
- An attitude so positive, it was contagious
- A great teammate, preferring others over himself
- Mentally tough, he'd play through some heavy pain
- Tenderhearted, he loved everyone
- Courageous, like few others I have known

In your journal today, evaluate this list in terms of how you stack up. If you fall short of the mark, there will never be a better time than right now to commit yourself to changing course, overcoming all excuses and living life with a passion that from this day forward, you will never be the same. Now pray and let Jesus lead you on to new heights! Rest in peace, Brooks, enjoy your wings. I'll see you soon.

Rock Speak
by Audie Lee Johnson III

In 1985, 1986, and 1987, Canyon Creek Christian Academy was a TAPPS state runner up. TAPPS was the largest governing body of private schools in Texas at that time. A great man by the name of Ron Binion was the head coach of the Cougars. Why would anyone leave such a situation? Well, the fact was that Canyon Creek Christian Academy was tied to a church, and the church split over controversy; hence, the school went into a tailspin of decline in enrollment, morale, and in every way you could think would be associated with such a situation. Enter Ted "Rock" Knapp (who had not been given all of the dirty details upon accepting the assignment). I remember as a seventh grader sitting there listening to this large bald man (who I considered to be the most intimidating person I had ever met at that early stage in my life) speak at the end-of-year sports banquet. I remember him telling his story of taking on and defeating a Cincinnati football powerhouse with a small private school just like ours. He proclaimed in his speech that that is exactly what we were going to do to Plano Senior High.

See, the Plano Wildcats were close to 5,000 students strong and coming off multiple state championships. I was thinking to myself, this is Texas. Texas plays the best football in the nation; Plano is the best in Texas and, therefore, the best in the nation. You have to understand the "thang" about Texas is that we brainwash ourselves from infancy into believing that we are just better than everyone else because we are from Texas.

I digress, so there was Rock exclaiming how we would soon be the best in the nation. Those words carried an impact, a lifelong impact on an impressionable teenager who didn't know well enough to argue. That's the impact coaches and mentors carry. Every word uttered has an impact, and it's an awesome responsibility. Fast-forward several years later. I was a senior, and Rock had long moved on to better situations. I know you are wondering, "How did the Plano thing turn out?" Not well, the church and school continued to decline in numbers, and Canyon Creek had gone from a state contender to barely being able to field a team. However, Rock's words and motivation were still in my ears. You see, the real message behind the fancy speech was the lesson of the fight rather than the victory. Regardless of the outcome, you battle, you pour every ounce of yourself into what you do: school, football, your job, fatherhood, being a husband, your Christian faith, it's how you live, as a warrior for all the right reasons. This is the lesson I learned from Rock, and it is the lesson that is so often missed in life: battle daily, battle for right, battle against wrong, battle for your principles, battle for your faith. Essentially, fight the good fight.

We practiced in a park across the street from the school, not glamorous at all. A cold northern had blown through, and it brought the rain. We were down to eight players for a six-man team. There were two games left. I remember vividly sitting on a knee, darkness had rolled in, and the rain was falling. Our coaches told us no one would blame us if we packed it in, and the reality was that if we did, that would be the end of the program. I thought back to Rock's inspirational words and to the lessons he had taught me through the years (he and my family remained lifelong friends, and he mentored me from a distance), and that night, we decided to battle. Memories of scores and plays fade, but what remains with me today was the character trait of perseverance, of the battle.

In 2001, I returned to Canyon Creek as a coach. We were state ranked for three consecutive years, and in 2009 and 2010, they won conssecutive state championships. I often think back to that night, that one rainy night: what would have happened if we had not decided to battle? What would have happened if I had not been taught and mentored to persevere? What if I had been taught that quitting was an option because things didn't go my way? What if I didn't have a mentor like Rock? What if from one speech I hadn't realized that this was a man I could follow? What if Rock had moved on and decided not to mentor? What if I had not gone into education as a result of Rock's mentoring? What if? What if? What if?

I would not be the man I am today. I would not be the husband I am today. I would not be the Christian I am today. I would not be the school leader I am today. When times get tough, I wouldn't know how to persevere, but rather, I would know how to quit. When life got hard, instead of facing the battle, I would retreat. When parenting becomes a grind, I would give in rather than instill discipline. Marriage quarrels would turn into separating situations rather than relationship binders. Life would suck!

Don't mistake what I am saying. It was not the words of the speech that started me on this journey over twenty-five years ago. It was the man behind the speech, the principles of the speech, and the lifelong impact that mentors have the opportunity to instill. Because of Rock's influence, I have the opportunity to help mentor thousands of students every year. I get to pass on a legacy of a man who my students will never meet this side of glory.

So great story, but what's the takeaway? It's simple; it's the Michael Jordan effect. To paraphrase Number 23, he said that he realizes that every time he goes into public, it may be the only time people get to see the great Michael Jordan. In realizing this, he has decided to be at his best at all times. As people in society, we should take that same approach and look for opportunities to impact for the positive. Let our words be our bond and realize that everything we say and do has an impact on who we are and how we affect others. One man forever shaped who I am today, and I will forever be grateful for his impact. It is an impact that is built out of a strong Christian faith. Football was the avenue, but it doesn't have to be your avenue. The point is find an avenue, be the mentor. Everyone needs a Rock, so I ask you, "Whose Rock are you today?"

> Blessed is the man who perseveres under trial, because when he has stood the test, he will receive the crown of life that God has promised to those who love Him.
>
> James 1:12 (NIV)

But one thing I do: Forgetting what is behind and straining toward what is ahead, I press on toward the goal to win the prize for which God has called me heavenward in Christ Jesus.

Phil. 3:13–14 (NIV)

Let nothing move you. Always give yourself fully to the work of the Lord, because you know that your labor in the Lord is not in vain.

1 Cor. 15:58 (NIV)

Rock here: Audie Lee Johnson has been a young man I have known now since he was in the seventh grade. His dad, Audie Sr., has been a great mentor in my life. The entire family has meant a great deal to my entire family. "Little" Audie is now all grown up, been a championship football coach, a championship husband and father. Today, he is a high school administrator in the Pearland, Texas, school district. I love him like a son, and my heart is blessed to know his life is fully committed to Jesus. My prayer today is everyone who ever reads this devotional be moved to mentor on behalf of the Good News of the Gospel of Jesus Christ.

Marc Stevenson

Hi, Coach! Some of the principles that I learned playing football for you:

First, let me say that I wasn't the football star. I loved the game and gave all I had, but I was just an average player on a great team. I returned kicks and punts and rotated in some on defense. The role of backup was difficult to accept as I excelled at baseball and basketball and was used to starting in sports. But I think I learned more about myself and teamwork because of it.

This leads me to the first principle I learned from you.

1. Principle #1. You don't have to be great to be a part of something great!

2. Principle #2. The journey is as important as the destination!

I knew the last game (the championship game that we won) would be the last football game I would ever play. That was a bit tough for an eighteen-year-old who loves football to accept, but I certainly didn't have the ability to play in college.

It ended so fast, but as I reflected, I realized that what would mean as much to me as the ring was all the wonderful sweet memories of practices, bus rides, teammates, and fun we had every day!

3. Principle #3. Vision matters!

I'll never forget your having us put tape on the ring finger that would one day wear the real championship ring (which I still have and cherish). Everyone knew exactly what the goal was. At first, it seemed like a lofty goal, maybe even a bit unrealistic, but something crazy happened, we started to believe it! And it happened!

Proverbs 29:18: "Where there is no vision, the people perish." The role of leadership is really simply vision-casting!

4. Principle #4. Demanding excellence in preparation produces excellent results.

You demanded that every practice, every film session, every workout be done with excellence. I'll never forget our warm-up routine before games. It was like a perfectly orchestrated performance in and of itself. Now I realize that it sent the message to the other team that if they are that perfectly in sync to get ready to play the game, we're in trouble when this thing starts.

It taught me that preparation shines through in the smallest of details.

That details matter!

5. Principle #5. Every person matters

You had the same expectation from the stars as you did from the third string water boy. It taught me that excellence and work ethic was required from everyone if the team would be great. And that laziness and low expectations, if accepted from any, would contaminate all! I've learned over the many years pastoring a church that every job, no matter how small, *must* be done with excellence. And while my playing field now is the church instead of the ball field, I demand excellence from every leader. Because it's the environment and climate that builds a great team.

Coach, I could literally go on and on about the many things I learned from your leadership.

I was just the short skinny kid, but my head and heart was open, and in the short time we spent together, I watched what a great leader could accomplish.

You have been one of the most impactive people in my life, and for that I say, thank you!

God bless you, Coach!

> Build your program on principles, not playbooks! You'll reach every player rather than just the starting line-up.
>
> —Rock Knapp

David Turner

The following is a letter received from Houston Christian High First Team All-State DE, David Turner. David transferred to Houston Christian from Ike, a huge public school with a long football tradition. He went on to a play at a high level at Lambuth University. Today, David teaches school and is a year away from becoming Dr. Turner (a PhD in English)! He is a Renaissance man and he is my friend.

Then I saw a tall, stocky, bald man, with these piercing gray-blue eyes. I thought he was Lou Ferrigno or something because compared to me, he was huge! We shook hands and he said, "Hi, I'm Coach Knapp." After fifteen minutes with him, I felt that Northwest might be a good fit for me. Coach Knapp was the type of man and coach you never wanted to disappoint. He had that effect on his players and coaches. I have never been a part of a team that was as united and supportive as this one was, even with the cultural differences. We all came together like on *Remember the Titans*. Although everyone wanted an opportunity to play, we never placed that ahead of the ultimate goal of winning games and, ultimately, a state championship. Never before had I been a part of a team where the coaches cared about your well-being on and off the field as much as Coach Knapp and the rest of the coaches did. They worked us physically and pushed us to the limit, and they challenged us to do our best academically, not only to stay eligible, but to make a brighter future for ourselves. Most of all, Coach Knapp fed us spiritually and modeled it for us the best way he knew how. It was in the way he treated us, his wife, his kids, his coaches, his coworkers, and his friends. Everyone loved Coach "Rock" Knapp. Was he perfect? Of course not, but he didn't try to be either, which made me respect him even more. He showed me how to make a mistake, own up to it, but always keep moving forward afterward. Coach Knapp went on to organize and coach the first annual Bayou Bowl, an all-star game that would help to showcase the talent from private schools all over the area, and I was invited to participate. He was also selected as

Coach of the Year along with many other well-deserved honors. I enjoyed the camaraderie and experience playing with other all-star players from other teams. It was equally thrilling to play the game at Rice Stadium in front of our families, friends, and college coaches. After the season, I won first team all-state and First Team all-district honors, and I owe all of that to Coach Knapp for taking a chance on me and believing in me. I received several scholarship offers and accepted one from Lambuth University at the last minute. I had verbally committed to Southern University in Baton Rouge, Louisiana, but I did not have my test scores in by the deadline, and they gave the scholarship to another recruit. Although I was initially disappointed, I was happy that my dream of playing college football and going to college was becoming a reality. I was invited to several open-tryouts for NFL teams, as well as personal workouts with the Titans and Jaguars, but I didn't get the opportunity to play on an NFL team. Today, I have made a successful career in education of over ten years. I have taught high school and college English. I received my master's degree in 2009, and I will graduate with my doctorate in early 2015. God has been good to me to place people in my life that will help me to get to where I am now. Coach Knapp was one of those people, and I thank God for the opportunity to play for him and to learn how to be a better player, but more importantly, a better man.

Teddy Knapp

Yes, he is my son. I have been the luckiest coach ever to have been able to coach both sons and for both to make first team all-state selections: Teddy in Maryland/DC/Northern Virginia and Nile here in the southern football Mecca of Georgia. Teddy was one of three great wide receivers I had in my thirty-year career, John Brooks and Hank Lankford being the other two. The acorn doesn't fall from the tree: my son is a Christian high school assistant football coach. I am glad for our memories.

Dad didn't have to ask me twice to be a contributor to this book. It is destined to be a best-seller! I remember many things about playing for my dad. I remember two-a-days in the Houston heat. I remember hours of studying film and sitting in the bleachers scouting other teams. I remember the military-style training and preparation. I remember being in the weight room every day of the summer. He always treated me like his son until we were on the field. Then I was just like everybody else. If I messed up, I ran. If I didn't get the job done, I got replaced. If I didn't put in my greatest effort, I got yelled at. I don't think I've ever said this out loud to him before, but I always admired him for that. It would be really easy to give your own kid a leg up on the competition, but he stuck by his rules: the best and hardest working players got the spot. After we left the field though, he was right back to being dad again. Every day on the way home from practice, he would tell me what he saw out of me. He would praise me when I did well, and he would tell me what I needed to do to improve when I failed. Football was always the one common love we shared.

The one story that does stand out is Homecoming 1998. It was my freshman year. I started in most of our packages at wide receiver. I also returned punts. We were scheduled to play St. Pius X, who at the time was ranked number 1 in the state in 4A. We were ranked number 1 in 3A. Both of us were undefeated so far. People told my dad he was crazy for scheduling them for homecoming. They said we didn't stand a chance. It's kind of funny to me. My whole life I grew up being with him at practices and film days. He always seemed to have that one game every year when people told him, "You don't stand a chance." I guess he used that as motivation, because 9.9 times out of 10, he won those games.

I still remember every day of practice that week. It was intense. We put in more time and work that week than I had ever seen him put in before. Starting on Saturday, Dad was in coaches' meetings and the film room all weekend, except for Sunday morning when we went to church, and then he was right back at it. When we started practice on Monday, you could tell there was something different about Dad, about all the coaches. We ran plays over and over and over until they were perfect. Even the scout team had to be perfect. There was no margin for error. We installed special plays just for this game. Being at home with Dad was a nightmare. All we did was watch film and talk about how we could win. He was so zoned in on that game. By the end of the week, the whole team bought into what Dad was selling, victory.

That year, St. Pius had a sophomore running back by the name of Yamar Washington. This kid was a monster. He was 205 pounds, fast, hit the hole hard, and was keen on running you over if you got in his way. He had rushed for over 150 yards in every game that year. His linemen were built like skyscrapers. Their coach, Chuck Faucette, who happened to be good friends with Dad, was as good as they get. The key to beating them was to shut down Washington. We put in a whole new defense just to stop this kid. There was no way they were going to come into out house and throw us a beating.

Our stadium by the railroad tracks was filled to the brim. There were people everywhere. Dad guestimated 4-5,000 paid fans. The game started. It was a battle. It was the hardest fought game I've ever been in. Both teams wanted it. It seemed like every time we scored, so did they. They scored with a few minutes left in the game, and it really sucked the life out of the team. During a timeout, a voice came out of the middle of the huddle; it was Dad. "Hey, you better suck it up and get your heads out of your butts. We worked too hard for this. And let me say right here and right now, I believe in you and I love you regardless of the outcome, but boys, this is your moment, your time, your destiny, now break this huddle and be the best football team in Texas!" That was all it took for us to explode! We drove the ball all the way down the field. We scored with thirty seconds left on the board to go up by three points. We kicked it off, and St. Pius had their final play. The final score was 31-28. I remember looking at the clock as it ticked down: 4, 3, 2, 1. As that clock ran down, I looked at my dad. He was looking at me too. I ran over and hugged him. As we were hugging, we started to jump up and down, and in that moment, I felt like his son on the field for the first time. All that work, all that time, all that preparation, and the thing that meant the most was those two or three seconds I had with my dad jumping around. A few seconds later, the whole team jumped in, and we had a great celebration of our victory. It was the most memorable experience from my entire football career. My dad is magical with that whistle around his neck, and now watching him live out all he taught us as he stands his ground against the pain and suffering of cancer. Rock Knapp, he is the greatest man I've ever known.

Mike Kershaw

If I had to choose the most influential football family of my thirty-year career, no contest, it would be the Kershaws: dad, Phil; sons, Kris and Mike. They did way more for me and my family than I ever did for them. I'll let them tell you their story, but I have to say Phil may be the savviest person I have ever known. He would be a world champion if he played chess. He is extremely analytical (always one step ahead) and a master problem-solver. And, schmooze man can he, schmooze (win people over in any situation). His support and counsel over the years had real impact on my success. His boys? Let me put it in one neat package that everyone can understand: with a Kershaw under center, I never lost a single game, half or quarter of football. Put that in your pipe. Kris and Mike were great talents, great leaders, and great football minds. Here is Mike writing his coach.

Where do I start? I first met Coach Knapp in Lancaster, California, at Antelope Valley Christian School when my brother moved down there. I don't really remember much about him then except he was an intimidating-looking guy. Also, he was kind of funny looking. My brother Kris had lots of stories about this man and really seemed to take to him. This coach kind of took on a Roman god-like persona from the stories I heard about his prior coaching stops and how many games and championships he had won. But this school had not won a game the year before, so how much could he really do for this team? Well, all he did was put a bunch of misfits from all over and mold them into an undefeated California state champion! Wow, this coach must be a coaching god, and then he was gone! During my first year with Coach Knapp (I followed Coach to Louisiana to play for him and live with his family), my new family allowed me to see a different side of him than most people saw. I was behind the scenes, behind closed doors. I was able to see the father and husband Coach was. Coach Knapp may put off that he is the king of his castle, but I think everyone really knows who runs the show, Shari. I have learned so much from him about being a father and husband, sitting back and watching him have devotions at night with his family, having discipline when the kids needed it, singing his gospel songs, and watching some show with this old nun lady on it. Of course, we watched a lot of football and sports as well. Some of the interesting things about Coach that he did or said were:

- Teddy, you better stop or I'll whip your butt, son!
- He vacuumed all the time, like every night. We went through a couple vacuums a year.
- Don't ever sit in his recliner! Ever!
- Loves him some Blue Bell ice cream.
- Drove his B2000 truck and still had New York license plates on it. He had been in three or four states after that. Time to change the plates!

- When he was on the phone with someone or leaving a message, he would always spell out his name. "This is Coach Knapp, K-N-A-double P."

Coach worked for his players like a dog trying to get them college scholarships. He made highlight videos, called coaches, and sent out transcripts, and in my case, even drove me to look at schools. This small 1A school that just started playing football had five players sign college scholarships to schools all over the country. This was no small feat, and the bulk of the credit has to go to Coach Knapp for all his hard work.

My short two years with Coach Knapp at WCA was a huge success on and off the field. We finished up 19-0, and I received a football scholarship to play at Western Colorado and won plenty of awards and honors. Did I mention that I did this at a playing weight of 145 pounds dripping wet! But I was a solid 145 pounds thanks to Shari's salmon patties and mac and cheese! Off the field, I learned things that when I was a college football coach, I taught my players, I learned parenting skills that I use today with my kids, and I learned how to try to be a great husband. Even though I was as stubborn as Coach sometimes and we had a couple dust-ups, my life will forever be changed because of Coach KNA double P! I love you!

Kris Kershaw

And now here is Mike's brother Kris Kershaw, who was the California Small School Player of the Year (lefty QB), played college football on the East Coast, and ended his career attempting to make the Toronto Argo's of the CFL. Kris was our captain, and to this day, I would trust him with all my being. They do not come better!

It's been twenty-two and half years since the AV Christian Eagles went 13-0 and won the state championship for California. I have always thought the story of that team deserves to be told because of what was accomplished with that group. We were for the most part a group of lost teenagers who were at a crossroad of choosing a right or wrong path. Drug dealers, arsonist, runaways, armed robbers, dropouts, to cover a few, all like a group of lost puppies looking for direction. This was the first time I met Coach Knapp, and he looked nothing like I pictured. He looked young and big enough to still play at some level, and I felt bad for him because he had to be thinking the same thing I was. This group did not pass the eyeball test. As I listened, I was amazed of the conviction he spoke with when he declared this team would go undefeated and win a state championship. Our first game was such a mystery. Most of the team had never played organized football before, so the nerves were high. They were escalated when we were watching our opponent warm up. They were an inner city school from Los Angeles that was much bigger and more athletic than we were. Coach was getting ready for the game as though he was about to strap up and play. He was so confident and I didn't understand why. Was he putting on a show to build us up, or was it from a twelve-year history of being in this position before and coming out on top? We started the game with the ball first, and I remember the first play was a play action pass to the tight end. As I was calling out the signals, I looked over to our bench and saw Coach Knapp with his hands in the air, screaming, "Touchdown! Here it comes!" Wow! As I dropped back, faked the handoff, I looked up to see a wide open receiver to throw it to for an easy touchdown. We went on to win, 56-6. We were on the front page of the paper the next day. It was the first time I have had my name in the paper since my birth announcement. Off the field was not going as well; we still had no practice field. We would drive around town looking for parks to practice at until we were kicked off, and there was also the financial stress that caused rumors that the school may not make it through the year. Coach Knapp appeared to us unfazed by all of the noise and uncertainty around us, keeping us focused on the next week's opponent.

We prayed a lot, which was different for a lot of us, before practice, during sometimes, and after. Coach led us and kept our focus on the job at hand through a focus and faith in Christ. God was going to provide no matter how things looked on the outside, and as the season continued, we started to believe that God was guiding us no matter what happened off the field.

As the wins started to pile up and we climbed the state rankings, we started to get some attention from the *Los Angeles Daily News* and the *Los Angeles Times*. How far could we go? Could we actually make a run at a state championship despite the fact we didn't have a permanent practice facility? We went into the playoffs undefeated as the number 1 seed according to the state rankings. We rolled through the playoffs by winning our first two games by fifty points, taking us to the state semifinal in Lone Pine. (Back to the sight of the passing tournament where we first bonded as a team.) This visit was a lot different though. Their offense and defensive lines outweighed us by fifty pounds a person. It was maybe fifteen degrees at kickoff, and the entire town was there to watch. There were people surrounding the field, and they were hissing and growling at us as we took the field. The game started off with us taking an early lead by throwing the ball on every play. They couldn't keep up with us until I took off on a scramble and got hit in the head, causing me to black out. I couldn't remember anything and was taken out. Coach Knapp kept his cool and put in the back-up who had next to no experience, not just during games but practice as well. Trey threw for 2 touchdowns and led us to a 40-12 win. It was easily one of the bravest performances of any player on that team. It was as if God rewarded him for his patience and character all year by saying, "You will not play much, but you will play one of the most important roles for this team to win a championship." The next week, we went on to win the state championship to finish the season, 13-0. Coach Knapp absolutely turned the opponent inside out with his game plan. I had a 22-25 game! We clobbered those poor saps, 54-28. Two of their scores came late in the fourth quarter. As that game started to get in our control and it was inevitable that we were about to win, I looked around the bench and admired what my teammates had accomplished. Coach Knapp predicted this six months earlier when it was uncertain that we could even field a team. We finished the year outscoring our opponents, 658-88. We also had numerous all-league and all-state honorees, as well as the state's coach of the year.

Coach Knapp was able to get the most out of his players by pushing us out of our comfort zone and beyond what we thought was possible. We developed a trust for each other that, "the guy next to me was going to do his job, so all I had to worry about was doing mine." The attention to detail in all of our practices from our stretching routine to the way we left the field once the game was over was what made us great. Coach Knapp had a vivid "vision of success" that showed in everything he did. He wanted each of us to be men of excellence; what an example! Never seen a guy love his players like Coach loved us.

Zander Hatcher

You want this guy to marry your daughter! He comes from a great family. I will love them all forever. Talk about smart, polite, talented, and a heart for others, all three Hatcher kids were cut out of the same fabric. Zman started at safety for two seasons.

There were so many good times it would be impossible to type and describe, but the thing that does not hit you until after you graduate is what tough really means. I had a coach that showed up to every practice every meeting every day while fighting his terminal cancer. The fact is that he could have thrown in the towel at any time, but showed what true character, true heart, true courage is all about. The man was a genius when it came to football, but where he means the most is not on the field. A high school football coach is special to everyone who plays. I am blessed to have known Coach Rock, and he will always be very special to my family. He brought some of the happiest times of my life, and after all the great football talk is said and done, he is a great husband, father, and a great friend. And he loved me—win, lose, or draw.

Dan Jones

Dan Jones is a Missouri boy and the best basketball coach I ever worked with. We had such a wonderful relationship. His best players played football, and my best players were on his roster. We were both about the kids. Dan is a godly man with such a tender heart. But this dude takes no prisoners when it comes to competing to win. Dan always found a way into the state rankings and made many runs at district and state titles. We were each other's biggest fan, and may I just say, Dan Jones is simply the best fisherman on the planet! Here is that e-mail.

Rock, I love you, man! I am honestly baffled sometimes at what God does, but in the end, he always gives me a peace and I am able to operate above the storm. I want you to know that I am so proud to say I am counted blessed to be a friend of yours. You inspire me every day to be better for these kids. The way you have persevered through this storm and the inspiration you have been to so many thousands is just short of unbelievable. Bro, I really want you to feel the love I have for you. I am praying continually for God to allow you to be with us a full lifetime! Praying for him to heal you completely from this sickness and the complications of it.

Phil Kershaw
The Commissioner Speaks
(Phil Kershaw was the commissioner of the CFL and the president of the Saskatchewan Roughriders)

In 1990, my oldest son Kris was looking to continue his education and football career in the United States. We lived in Regina, Saskatchewan, which for those not familiar is in the Canadian prairies north of Montana.

As a result, it was decided he would go to live in Lancaster, California, with his grandmother and attend a small Christian school called AV Christian School, entering his sophomore year.

In meeting with the founder of the school, Dr. David Ralph, he told me that he had hired a dynamic young coach for their football program named Ted Knapp.

Kris was excited because as an aspiring quarterback, he was looking forward to being able to step up his game and also step up with the anticipation of the better competition he would experience in the US.

He wasn't disappointed. Ted was not only a great coach and mentor of quarterbacks, but was an amazing football talent who was able to blend innovative coaching strategies with a God-given gift of being able to communicate and connect with young players. The results were off the charts. The 1990 AV Christian Eagles won the CIF small school football title, a huge accomplishment for a new fledgling Christian school that had just started an athletic program.

For Kris, the results couldn't have been better. Thanks to Ted's coaching and great receivers, like Craig Cieslik and Jason Allred, he was able to put up impressive numbers, throwing thirty-three touchdown passes, being voted California's small school player of the year, and getting write-ups in the *Los Angeles Times* and *Daily News*.

Sadly, Ted's tenure at AV Christian only lasted one year. Kris continued to excel during his junior and senior year, but without Ted, no more championships were to be had.

However, this was not to be the end of the adventure for the Kershaw and Knapp families. In 1993, Ted had relocated to Westminster Christian School in Opelousas, Louisiana, and was interested in knowing if Kris's younger brother Mike, who had followed him to California, would be interested in becoming his quarterback down in Acadiana (ironically, Cajuns originated in Canada's east coast). Mike took the invitation and had two great unbeaten seasons in the Deep South and was able to trade that opportunity into a football scholarship to Western State in Colorado, then Delta State in Mississippi, leading them in 1998 to the NCAA Division 2 playoffs for the first time in their history.

Looking back, there is no doubt that Ted was a driving force in their football careers. Kris went on and was a starting quarterback at Salisbury State in Maryland and then was drafted by the Toronto Argonauts of the Canadian Football League.

Mike not only had a successful college career at Delta State, but returned to his alma mater to coach for six seasons, plus served as a guest coach at training camp for the Canadian League champion Montreal Alouettes.

All of that was amazing, and obviously, as a father, I was very proud that the boys were able to come from the Great White North and make their mark in the mecca of football in the States. However, now with the benefit of time and hindsight, the real important part of this experience is what having Ted as a coach and mentor did for their character and preparation for life after the cheering has ended.

That was Ted's greatest contribution: giving them the life lessons of responsibility, commitment, industry, and integrity.

A person should never underestimate the impact that a strong Christian man can have on young boys and getting them on the right road in life.

I have been blessed in life to meet many amazing, talented people, but I always will be grateful to Ted for being there when taking the scary step of letting both of my sons go south and, believe me, not without some trepidation on my part.

Frankly, God was looking out for our family, and there was a godly man at the other end to watch over and lead them.

Today as adults, Kris and Mike are husbands, fathers, and successful business people. I have to be honest, Ted Knapp deserves a lot of credit for that, and what greater gift can a father ask from another person?

Thanks, Ted, and God bless you, Shari, and your family forever.

I read this and went immediately to my knees, thanking God for directing my ministry in such a way that Christ was the central focus of my relationships with thousands of young men and *not* the game of football or winning or climbing the ladder of success. I was driven first and foremost to impact each boy to become the full specific potential for which God created them. And may I also say with great, great joy, I have watched as Christ has become the Lord of Phil Kershaw's life! So, Coach, keep first things first as you invest your time and talent into your boys today. Love them unconditionally, come alongside them, and help them dream big dreams and teach them to follow Christ and love Christ above all others. Winning games must take a secondary role to winning surrendered lives for the Savior of all creation.

Hank Lankford

Hank is now, and forever will be, one of the boys I love like a son. Hank is one of the kindest, most loyal, and most dependable men on the planet. He was one of three receivers (Teddy Knapp and John Brooks, being the other two) that never dropped a ball in a game. He was such an important reason for our state title that year. He remains very important to me, and I look forward to our next fishin' trip!

I have to travel back to the year 1980 to relive one of the best years of my life. I remember it as if it were yesterday. It was the day I was to be at Newnan Christian School to set up my schedule as a freshman before school actually started. I don't remember much about my schedule, but I do remember getting to school and seeing a man I had never met before holding a clipboard. He greeted me, introduced himself as Coach Knapp, said we were starting a football team, and he wanted me to participate. I did not hesitate at all; I wanted to play. I had never played organized football before, but had played backyard football my entire life. I just knew how much fun I thought it would be to play, and I immediately was drawn to Coach Knapp; everyone was.

We started practicing in a vacant lot behind a BBQ joint in Newnan. I think only two of us had ever played any kind of organized football. I am not sure how I ended up as a receiver, but I loved catching the football and it seemed to come naturally to me. We worked hard at every practice, and Coach Knapp pushed us until we knew every play to perfection. His attention to detail and perfect execution of every play was expected at every practice and paid off in our game performance.

I remember lots of wins that season and especially our come from behind win in the state championship game. We were down

14-0 at the end of the first half and came back to win the game 30-14. It was a magical season that I will never forget, but we certainly learned more than football that year.

Coach Knapp taught us a lot of life lessons that year. Through the game of football, we learned values and character traits that helped make us into the men we are today. Coach showed us what respect really means. He taught us to respect our leaders as well as each other as teammates. The common respect we shared helped us reach our goal that year of winning a state championship. The character traits and manners we learned on a daily basis have become invaluable to us as husbands, fathers, sons, brothers, employees, and employers. When I find myself in the fourth quarter of a tough situation, I am reminded to put on my chin strap, square my shoulders, and go forward with courage until the finish. I may not always win, but I find victory as long as I have done my best, which is what Coach Knapp always taught us.

I recently got to spend some time with Coach Knapp and Mrs. Shari at the beach for dinner, and then I took Coach on a fishing excursion. We had a great time. As always, Coach wanted to catch up with what was going on in my life and tell me how proud he was of me. I finally got him to do some talking about his battle with cancer. As I listened to him talk about his struggle with the disease, I realized that he is still using the same "stay strong until the finish" attitude that he tried to instill in us back in 1980. His example of courage and love for others remains the driving force of my life.

John Brooks

John Brooks is a highly successful State Farm agent; he has his own agency that he and his wife service clients from in Jacksonville, Florida. Everything John touches seems to turn to gold. He just took up golf some years back, and the next thing ya know, he's shooting in the 70s. I can testify to his football skill and contribution during our two-year undefeated run. He was unbelievable: never dropped a pass in practice or a game! He was smart, coachable, and always hungry to see the ball coming his way. In fact, John should have gotten 50-75 more balls his senior year. We just had so many weapons it prevented him from racking up huge numbers. Read this story from the player's perspective. It sure proves God will bring your dreams to life and in a much bigger way than we could have imagined!

God Answers Prayer

I woke up every morning after having the same dream: playing high school football and then playing college football. But every morning, the same reality hit me: I was going to a private school that did not play tackle football. My mom worked for the school, and per school policy, all her children had to attend. This meant my ultimate dream of playing college football was not going to happen, but the dream kept visiting me each night. After sharing my dreams with my parents, it was decided I should pray and ask God to enable my school to start a football program. This is crazy, I thought. There is no way this will happen. For the next two years, I prayed the same prayer and had the same dreams. To say I gave up on the idea is an understatement, but I prayed anyway just to cover my bases. I was called into a meeting one spring afternoon and was introduced to a man who was coming to my school to start a tackle football program. The man told us the flags were gone, and we would compete for championships and told us how we would make history. I was so grateful to God for answering my prayer that my mind raced with these possibilities: Who is this guy? Why would he come here? If he is coming here, how good could he be? We don't have a weight room, uniforms, or pads; how is this going to happen? I have found that this is often the case when God gives us the desires of our hearts, we tend to doubt more that be excited.

The Lion or the Gazelle

> Every morning in Africa, a gazelle wakes up and knows that it must run faster than the fastest lion or it will be killed. Every morning, a lion wakes up and knows that it must run faster than the fastest gazelle or it will go hungry. It does not matter whether you are a lion or a gazelle, when the sun comes up, you better be running.

Westminster Christian Academy was a private school with less than 150 students in its high school. It had never had a tackle football program, so everything was new. The king of the start-ups was Ted Knapp. How do you get kids to learn how to play football? You tell them the above quote day in and day out. I had to learn football 101 since I had never played before. Everything was new: the pads, the helmets, the stances, and the heat. That first spring, we spent an entire week learning the correct tackling positions. We installed maybe fifteen plays and would spend an entire day running the same play. Still, the above quote was told to me over and over. How Coach Knapp had the patience to do this, I will never know. I own a business today, and the hardest thing to do is take an employee who knows nothing about my industry and teach him everything I know. It is a painstakingly slow process, and Coach Knapp was doing this with thirty boys all at once. But I knew it then and I know it now: something was building. I did not know what, but I knew something special was happening. That's the thing with God: when you are in his time and his plan, you have this unlimited courage to keep walking in faith.

That first spring practice was basic football 101. Then came the fall, and we were all introduced to two-a-days: practice in the morning, practice in the afternoon. August in South Louisiana, the temperature is 90 by 8:00 am with 100 percent humidity, but what fun I was having. We had no idea what was going to happen when we actually played, but we kept practicing, learning, and *running*. We were taught to always run back to the huddle, to the sideline, no matter what. If you didn't, you ran more. Gassers after a two-hour practice till you puked were an everyday occurrence. I did not know if we would be the lion or the gazelle that season, but I knew I was not going to be outrun by anyone.

    Finally, the season came and we won our first game. Then on the Tuesday before our second game, our starting quarterback got suspended for some reason I can't remember at this time. Coach called me into his office and told him I was starting at quarterback on Friday night. I was the backup quarterback, but I hated the position and was much better playing wide receiver. To say I was nervous was an understatement, and to say Coach Knapp dumbed down the playbook was a bigger understatement. Our starting quarterback ended up playing college football in Mississippi, had a great career, and coached in college for many years. Now comes Friday night: nowhere to hide and it's all on me. A kid who dreamed of playing football and in the second game of my life, I am starting at quarterback. God is either really cool or really cruel. Somewhere during the first half, I drop back for a pass and I throw an interception. Not a great feeling, I have let my team down, myself down, and I have done it in front of all these fans in the stands. Coach calls another passing play. *Don't blow it again*, is all I am thinking. I take the snap and roll to my left. The wide receiver on the left side runs straight down the line of scrimmage to the right. I stop and I can't see my receiver and I don't know if he is there, but I throw to where he is supposed to be and get hit and go down to the ground. Nothing, what happened, then, yelling, oh, no, another. I get up and see Joel Comeaux running into the end zone. Wow! What a feeling! God is really cool. We won the game; I got a game ball!

    That game sticks with me because during the first half, I was the gazelle being caught by the lion. However, during the second half, I was the lion and I was victorious. This is the same in the game of life. You will be down one minute and up the next. The thing that matters is that you keep getting back up, tears and all, every time and try to do better. As I write this now, I have a huge smile on my face, remembering the tears but not quitting, trying again and throwing a touchdown to seal a win late in the game. If this were a movie script, Hollywood would say it was too unbelievable, but it happened. However, I was to learn many more Hollywood scripts over the next two years.

My first year of playing tackle football was incredible. We went undefeated and even made *USA Today* as being the only school in the country to start a tackle football program, play a varsity schedule, go undefeated, and win a conference championship. Impossible, yes, probable no, but with God, the impossible is possible to ordinary people. As we entered year 2, everyone, and I mean everyone, told us it was a fluke and could not be repeated. I don't remember thinking we would be great, but I do know that my teammates and I had a confidence that was not there a year before. Not arrogance, Coach Knapp would never allow that, but confident that we could play with anyone and that second year we did. Westminster, at the time, was a 1A school, the smallest division of high school football. All we heard was that we played nobody this and nobody that. You tell Coach Knapp that long enough, and he will make things happen. We started the year 6-0 and we were rolling. We found out the next Monday that Coach Knapp scheduled a game with Live Oak High School, a 3A high school, for Friday night. Our scheduled opponent had called to forfeit, so we needed a team to play. Big boys, here we come. All week long, all we heard was how big they were and how we had to execute our game plan. Did we ever—we won the game, 49-14. Simply put, we had a coach who was better than theirs, and Coach Knapp simply outcoached the other team. He put us in the right formation, called the right play, and all we players had to do was execute, which we did. Now we had something really special going on, and we all knew how good we were playing.

We had a bye week the next week, and we were looking forward to it until we showed up at practice on Monday. Coach told us we would be playing Southern Lab, which is the high school on the Southern University campus and is their feeder school for their football program. I remember a couple of things from this game. First, Coach showed us the first ten minutes of *Patton*, where General Patton gives his famous speech to his troops. Second, we ran out onto the field and it was huge. Southern Lab played at Southern Stadium, home to Southern University Football Team. The stadium held almost 25,000 people. The third thing I remember is Southern Lab entering the stadium. They walked on the track around the whole field, clapping, yelling, and pointing at us, trying to intimidate us. I was not nervous, just excited, but man, Southern Lab was big and they were fast. This was David versus Goliath. The entire state knew we were playing this game, and everyone knew we would lose. However, with God the impossible is an everyday occurrence. We were up 26-7 at half time, and we ended up winning 29-14. Not even close, and it is still to this day my favorite football game. I have scored many touchdowns in my life, but I was fortunate to catch the first one of this game on a play that showed from the start we had a better coach than they did. After the game, Coach said a few things that have always stuck with me: he gave credit to God for the win and then he credited the character of our team. He then said, "At the beginning of the year, I thought we would be a good team, now I know that we have a great team." Is God cool or what!

We ended the year with another article in *USA Today* and went undefeated. In two years of tackle football, I was 21-0. Five guys from that team went on to play college football. One of my teammates received a full ride to play football at the University of Notre Dame, having only played two years of high school football. Father God answered the unimaginable prayer of a little boy to be able to play tackle football at a school that did not have a tackle football program. Father God brought Coach Knapp to my little school, and we went undefeated. I learned that there are times in life when I was going to be the gazelle, but I needed to get back up, *every time*, and try harder to be the lion. I learned that with God the impossible is routine and that David does beat Goliath. I learned that God uses ordinary people who are willing to humble themselves and ask God to move mountains and he will move them. I learned that Father God answered my dream to get a college scholarship to play college football from as far back as I could remember, and he answered it in the most action-packed Hollywood type of way. We serve an awesome, powerful, imaginative God. Never stop asking because you will be amazed at the ways he will answer.

Tim Pullin

Tim was my QB on the Landmark Christian Patriots 1984 NACA National Championship team. He had little natural ability. Tim was a kid who played within his talent, never made mistakes, and by the middle of the season, had developed real skill and provided the leadership from under center to execute the highly developed offensive packages. Today, he is Captain Pullin of the Alabama State Patrol. He supervises all other troopers from Lanett, Alabama, all the way to Montgomery. Maybe you'll meet him one day while speeding to get to an Auburn game!

It was a late night in the fall of 1984 when some of the fellows (Jimbo, Hobert, and Mike) and I were all out cruising the Atlanta highway. Like most teenagers, we got bored after some time, so we decided we would do some self-entertaining by doing something we had done several times in the past, rolling. No, this is not your typical rolling, toilet paper and trees. This type of rolling involved trash cans on wheels, a pickup truck, and some bored teenagers. The objective was for the truck driver to pull up beside a house with its trash can out at the road for pickup, and the fellows in the bed of the truck to grab the can and drag it down the road until optimum speed was reached—generally, 35 plus MPH. At the most opportune time, the fellows would let the trash can go and see how far the trash could be strewn. We had done this many times in the past without a hitch. On this particular night, we decided to take my truck. Yep, the one painted like four different colors because of the mismatched parts (yellow bed, green door, etc.) and probably the only one with a riding lawnmower in the back. Things started out pretty good with a few good rolls and a lot of litter. After a while, we petered out and decided to stop at the Zippy Mart just down the street from the school and Coach's house. While there, we enjoyed a cool drink and few rounds of the video games. As we started to leave, there they were, Montgomery's finest sitting across the street from the Zippy Mart, eyeing that old truck of mine. So being the smart young fellows we were, we thought we could wait them out—ten minutes, fifteen minutes, twenty minutes go by, and still no action. They remained steady on my old truck. Finally, we looked out the window and they were gone. We made our fast break northbound on Perry Hill Road, past Coach's house, trying to get to our teammate Donnie's house. With the driveway in sight, so were the blue lights in my rearview mirror. We pulled over just north of Coach's house and south of Donnie's. The nice officers approached my truck asking for the usual stuff, which I gave them. Well, then the grilling came.

"So, fellows, what have you all been doing tonight?"

"Nothing, officer, just playing video games and out riding around."

"Really, you think you can explain the trash cans and all the litter?"

"No, sir, I don't know what you're talking about." All along I'm thinking no one can ID us, so we are going to get away with it. Then out of the corner of my eye, I see a vehicle pull up and stop. I see the driver step out, and I'm thinking, *Oh, crap, it's a witness*. It wasn't a witness, but to our demise, it was Coach Knapp. He very calmly talked the officers into turning us over to his authority. "Gentlemen, if you will release the fellows to me, I can promise you won't have this problem again, and you won't have any more problems, I can assure you." Well, needless to say, practice for the next several weeks was very strenuous. There were days I puked and puked and thought I would die. Coach was more interested in us off the field than he was on the field. His influence left us all better Christian men.

I give this true life lesson as I reflect on where I am today because of Coach Knapp. At the young age of fifteen, I lost my father and I always looked up to Coach as a father figure. He took this true life experience and used it to help mold me into the person I am today, and it has even help me in my chosen profession, as I serve the citizens of Alabama proudly as a captain in the state troopers.

Troy McHenry

Let me introduce you coaches out there to Troy McHenry. Here is a rare statement: Troy never once needed to be corrected on or off the field in two years! He was the most polite and respectful player on the team with both coaches and players. Troy has quite a love for the Lord, as does his entire family. He was an honor student, started both ways, and as you are about to see, he was my starting point guard and gave a new meaning to the word *speed*. Just so you fully understand his letter, I did something during that season I had never done before (I actually coached six years of basketball and finished with one state title, two state runner-ups, and four region championships and an overall 98-28 record).

Anyway, on this night, we were playing the number 1 ranked team in the state, and I got a crazy idea. We won the opening tip, and Troy dribbled at the center circle for seven minutes and fifty-five seconds. Our opponent just stood in their 2-3 zone the entire time until the last five seconds when they attacked Troy. We set a rear screen for our sharp-shooting wing Huggy Voitier, and he squared up and drained the trey—3-0 at the end of one quarter. We came out the second, third, and fourth quarters and ran like the wind. Our guests from Baton Rouge seemed completely exasperated as we dominated and beat the state's best by twenty plus points. Troy had ice in his veins to go with Jesus in his heart!

Perseverance:

Seven minutes and fifty-five seconds into the first quarter, and Troy McHenry passes the rock to Huggy Voiter on the wing to drain a three pointer. First quarter score: WCA-3, Jimmy Swaggart Christian Academy-0.

Okay, let's back up to the week prior in preparation for one of the biggest games in our basketball season (1993–1994). Within our Christian school league, we were always considered one of the weakest teams on the schedule. During my freshman and sophomore year, our road trips consisted of us running "motion" for most of the night and getting creamed. Unfortunately, we had grown accustomed to contending for fourth place in our division. Ahead of us were LCA, Jimmy Swaggart's High School and North Side Christian (another rival). So let's move into my junior year. Coach "Rock" Knapp arrives on the scene and an immediate attitude change takes place. From the early summer months, he began to instill within us a passion for excellence—leaving it all on the court (regardless of the sport). Since we had a small student body and even smaller pool of athletics to choose from, we all played every sport. He taught us the art of mental preparation before battle, visualizing every play before it took place and understanding exactly what our role was and then execution. He made sure we were in the best physical shape of our lives. I vividly remember his sitting in the bleachers with his coffee mug in hand, whistle in mouth, and our running what seemed like an endless amount of lines (during deer hunting season when most of the players wished they were on their deer stand). So back to the storyline, the week prior to our playing Jimmy Swaggart's high school in our brand-new gym, Coach began to reiterate a brand of mental toughness we had not been previously introduced to. Each practice got a little bit harder; each drill drove us to knowing the floor and trusting each other and our specific role on the team. By Tuesday's night game time, we had already won the game in our mind. Tuesday evening after we had suited up in our new uniforms, we were all sitting in Coach's office with the lights off gearing up. The moment had finally arrived. The music begins to play our introduction into a standing room–only gymnasium filled with excitement. The door opens, and we storm out into the smoke, running our lap around the entire court, circling the opponent, and falling into a figure 8 warm-up drill. With just a quick glance, we can see the opponent trying not to look, but they have to, and when they do, we see it in their eyes. After the announcement of the line-up and a customary greeting, it's game time, baby. We win the jump ball, and I immediately run to get the pass. Coach had already called the play he wanted us to run before we left the locker room. I'm standing at the half-court circle, dribbling the ball from my left hand to my right. The opposing team is standing on all four blocks, waiting for us to attack; only problem is we were waiting for them to attack. Our play only went into full swing once they moved to guard us (which they did not). So here we stand at a stalemate (so you think). I'm dribbling the ball at half court, glancing back at Coach Knapp, and he gives me the nod to stand my ground. The crowd is standing on their feet cheering, waiting in anticipation, waiting to see what will happen. My dad (Mr. Mega Horn Man) is doing his famous growl. Seven minutes and thirty seconds, this scene does not change. With thirty seconds left in the quarter, the coach for the opposing team signals for them to come out and play the ball. I dribble to my right and dish the ball to Huggy on the wing. With no hesitation, he drains a three. They immediately try to run the length of the court and score, to no avail. Yes, sir, you guess it: game over. Everything we had prepared for weeks leading up to this game came to fruition in one quarter.

Lesson learned: Hebrews 12:1—If we had not put off all the past mishaps and disappointing seasons, we would not have valued the true meaning of persevering through trying times. We didn't understand the lessons being taught during practice, but they came to life during game time and have stayed with me some twenty years later. Trials will come as they are meant to test our faith and see where we truly stand. I have learned and remembered that I have to have a base so that I am not swayed from left to right, to stand firm in God's truth. Just as I would take a quick glance at Coach to make sure we were on the right course, you must keep your eyes fixed on the ultimate light house—Jesus Christ. He will never lead you astray. The closer you draw to him, the further along you will move in his will and defeat naysayers that try to get you off course or disrupt the game plan predestined for you.

"The race is not [always] to the swift, nor the battle to the strong" (Ecclesiastes 9:11, NIV).

Craig Cieslik

Craig Cieslik was the top receiver in the state of California his senior season. He was 6'3" and 185 and could jump and run with the skill of James Lofton. Trust me, he had that level of talent. He is one of the best up-and-coming head high school coaches on the West Coast. He is a popular clinician and quite the innovator offensively. Craig is the model of overcoming hardship to thousands. He has a severe speech impediment that would keep 99 percent of the population away from teaching and coaching, not Craig. He is a hero and champion to those who dream big.

—◦◦◦—

My life changed forever when I met Coach Knapp in the summer of 1990. Coach Knapp had just been hired to be the head football coach at one of the worst football programs in the state of California. The school was Antelope Valley Christian (AVC). It is located in Lancaster, California. I was going to be a senior in high school, and I got in some trouble my junior year at a different high school in the area. My father wanted my brother Chad and myself to change schools. Chad was going to be a junior. He said we both had to go to the same school, and we both had to agree on the decision. AVC the year before was 0-10 in football and struggled. They were the laughing stock of the entire state. The school I attended my junior year, along with my brother, was their crosstown rival, and we always beat them in every sport. We loved playing AVC; it was always seen as a stats game. My brother and I were three-sport athletes and wanted to go to a school where we could continue to be successful and continue to win.

When I was in the eighth grade, I had to do a project on what I wanted to accomplish by the time I graduated from high school. The teacher said she would mail us our work when we were about to graduate from high school in four years. At the top of my list was to win a CIF Championship in football. I also wanted to be an All-CIF player in football and in basketball, another love of mine. CIF is the California Inter-Scholastic Federation. It is the governing body for high school sports in the state of California. My dreams were to be a state champion in football and a standout football player in California.

I never thought in my wildest dreams that I would end up going to AVC for my twelfth grade year. That would have been the last school I would have chosen to go to! But God had different plans for me. My brother Chad stopped by AVC in June of 1990 to talk to their brand-new football coach, a guy named Ted "Rock" Knapp. Coach Knapp was hired at AVC on June 1, 1990. Coach Knapp had an amazing winning percentage and had won several state championships, and he was promising the same at AVC. When Chad stopped in to talk to him, Chad came home bragging about Coach Knapp—he was sold! He then explained his conversation with Coach Knapp and told my dad that he wanted to transfer to AVC. Chad told my dad and me, "Coach Knapp said we will win a CIF Championship this year!" I was laughing hysterically. I told my father and brother, "This is AVC, the worst football program around (0-10). There is no way you're going to win a CIF Championship." I begged and pleaded with my father to not listen to my brother. My dad found my brother's conversation very compelling and said I had to go talk to Coach Knapp. I argued with my father for hours, and in the end, he told me I had to go with Chad in the morning and talk to Coach Knapp.

So off we went in the morning to go talk to Coach Knapp. As soon as I walked in Coach Knapp's office on this tiny campus without a real football field, I was sold. There was an aura about Coach Knapp that just drew you in immediately. He was very intimidating to me and to countless other players. He was a very muscular bald man. I was a tall, slender high school kid. Coach Knapp started to talk to me about my hopes and dreams for my senior season. He told me that he would do everything he could to help me and the AVC football team be the best in the state! He told me all my hopes and dreams would come true if I played for him. Coach Knapp also told me what he was going to do at AVC and how he was going to make the football team CIF State Champions in his first year there. He said we will go from 0-10 to 14-0. I was sold on Coach Knapp's vision. Coach Knapp was a godly man who was very strict but very fair. Coach Knapp also had a great sense of humor and just inspired you to show up each and every day and work as hard as you could! This meeting with Coach Knapp that I fought and argued not to go to ended up being one of the best decisions I have ever made in my life. This meeting in Coach Knapp's office would change my life forever.

Once practice started, we had a makeshift weight room. We stored everything in a container and had to drag it out every day to weight lift. We practiced on a baseball field. The field had holes in it, so you had to be very careful. The facilities were at a church, and the high school itself was just a few years old. The permanent school was being built across town. During the football season, our new school was all portable trailers. Even our cafeteria was a portable trailer, and our locker room was a portable trailer, even our weight room. We couldn't put down weights too hard or they could go through the floor. To those of us who played there, we didn't know anything different. It was paradise for us, and Coach Knapp had sold all the players on the dream of being CIF Champions. If we had to lift weights and get dressed outside in the hallways, all of us would have done it. The school's football field wasn't completed either that year, so we had to all get rides across town, about fifteen minutes to an elementary school. Nobody complained. This is just how our life was and so we all did it. When we got to the elementary school, we would have to climb over or squeeze through the gates and then go and practice on their soccer field, which was also a softball and baseball field. My entire senior season we never practiced on one-lined football field, but somehow, we all made it work and made it work greatly! Our team had no home field for Friday night games. We played fourteen away games that season. Our home field was the local college: Antelope Valley College. Coach Knapp worked us hard and instilled in our team a sense of unity, passion, and togetherness that inspired us all to give it everything we had each and every single day. Coach Knapp also had just one assistant coach. His name was Coach Jay Elliott. They both worked great together and were the perfect partnership for our team! Both coaches had outstanding values, and I feel so blessed that I was able to know them both and play for them both.

During the 1990 season, it was a season that will never be forgotten by the AVC football team and community. We had an outstanding record of 14-0 and went on to win the CIF State Championship. I also had the honor to be chosen an All-CIF player. Both of my goals and dreams came true in the same year, thanks to Coach Knapp. I also got to win a championship with my brother! I owed him a big thank you! It has been one of the highlights of my life and one of the best times in my life. I am so thankful that God brought Coach Knapp into my life and the lives of my teammates that year. His incredible vision and work ethic made AVC Champions.

To this day, I have a strong love and enduring friendship and admiration for Coach Knapp. My dad still says he's the best high school football coach he has ever seen. I think I speak on behalf of everybody who has ever had the privilege to play for Coach Knapp that once you know him and play for him, you will never forget him! He just has that kind of impact on everybody's life he is around and is involved in. My own head coaching style to this day is highly based on the things I learned from Coach Knapp and his examples of selfless love, discipline, structure, accountability, and a love for your teammates who you go to battle with each and every play.

Even though I have not played for Coach Knapp for over twenty years, I have learned so much and continue to learn so much from him through the years by talking to him and meeting with him. He has helped me get many coaching jobs. As I grow older and more mature, I have so much respect for the wonderful husband, father, and grandfather that Coach Knapp is. It seems like whatever he puts his mind and heart to, he becomes the best at it. Coach Knapp has always inspired me and guided me throughout my life for the past twenty-three years. He has been like a second father to me and a lot of other men he has coached and become a part of their lives forever also. After my very first meeting with Coach Knapp and then after playing for him my senior season, I was so inspired by him that I wanted to go into teaching and coaching football. All the accomplishments I have achieved as a coach, I owe to what I learned and continue to learn from Coach Knapp. His battle with two types of cancer has been inspirational for thousands of people around the country. Coach Knapp's courageous spirit and faith in God has inspired me to live each day to the fullest and always see things in a positive light. I have also learned from him that whether it's a 0-10 program or two types of cancer, you fight and you give everything you have each and every single down. You do all that you can to become a winner on and off the field. This has made me become a better husband, brother, son, friend, and person.

When we depart this world, the only thing that is left of us is our character—who we were, what we did in our lifetime that gets passed down from generation to generation. I would have to believe that one of Coach Knapp's many legacies will be that he acted, worked, and treated people like a champion. That is something we all wish and hope can be said for ourselves one day when we depart this earth also. It is very rare in life that you meet somebody, and no matter how nice or how gifted they are, there is always some fault you can find in them. I think that is just human nature. It's truly amazing that for the past twenty-three years, my brother, my father, and I have never had anything negative to say about Coach Knapp. Nothing! Whenever we talk about Coach Knapp, it's always about what a great husband, father, grandfather, football coach, and friend he has been. That speaks volumes about the impact Coach Knapp has had on people and the impact he has had on my family. This is so rare to find. When Coach Knapp finally leaves this world some day for heaven, you need to bury his whistle with him because there will never be another like him!

Dale Moore

We'll end with one more. Here is a memory from many years ago from one of my very dearest friends, Dale Moore. Dale was an opposing coach who I fell in love with the first time we had a conversation. He was a shrewd coach and great with his boys. His love for the Lord was magnified by his good heart, a heart as big as Texas.

Being Real

It was the summer of 1982. I had traveled all the way from Texas to Fort Bluff Camp in Dayton, Tennessee, for the NACA All-Star Football Game. I had brought three high school players. We would have two-a-day practices through Thursday and then the East versus West game on Friday night. It was the first morning practice, probably around nine o'clock. It was hot and steamy with the practice field still wet with dew. We had divided up into groups and were going through drills. Normally, at a camp like this, the first morning is noncontact. You just want to have a look at your players in pads and try to determine who will play where. We were all from small private Christian schools from all over the nation and did not know that much about our players. We had no Internet in those days, and it took some time to evaluate players. The coaches and players were kind of quietly going about their business. About that time, at the opposite end of the field, I began to hear pads popping, a whistle blowing, and this big, booming voice calling out instructions and commands to his players. As we say in Texas, "They were already into it." This guy meant business, and he was relaying that to his kids and they were responding. I didn't know who this guy was, but I already liked him and knew I wanted to meet him. At that moment, I could sum him up in one word, "Passion." I asked one of the other coaches if they knew who he was. They said, "Yeah, that's

Ted Knapp." He was coaching the other team, and I knew we were in trouble. Come Friday night, those kids are going to be ready to play.

That was my first knowledge of Ted Knapp. Later that week, I met Ted, and we became instant friends. It was more than just the love of football that we shared. It was that special bond between two Christian brothers. There was much more to him than just football. He had a great passion for the gospel and directing young men to give their lives to Christ. He was also what I call real. He was the same on the field and off the field, in front of the kids and in private. As we say here in Texas, "What you see is what you get." There was no phoniness about him. I was encouraged by that. I was a young Christian and inexperienced as a coach and teacher at a very small private Christian school. Many times, when I would attend events with other schools and spend time with other coaches or teachers, I would find myself feeling like I did not belong. They had all the right Bible answers for every issue and appeared to be very successful at living the Christian life. If they saw what they thought was a chink in your armor, they had the answer and were quick to set you straight. I began to think, "Something's wrong with me. I don't have all the answers, and I mess up on a regular basis." I later found out that many of those people lived two lives, one in front of the world and a totally opposite one in private. Meeting Ted was like a breath of fresh air for me. Here was a Christian brother who was open and had nothing to hide. He was just Ted. I saw some of the same struggles in him that I was dealing with, yet he just continued to walk the walk day after day, and I have since observed, year after year no matter what life brings.

Last year, in December 2012, my wife and I drove down to Houston to see Ted and Shari and some of his grown-up children. He was there for the Rock Knapp Bayou Bowl, an annual all-star private school football game named after him. He went out on the field to speak to the players before the game and to make the honorary coin toss. He had to go out by golf cart since cancer has ravaged his body and the simple process of walking is extremely painful for him. I stood there on the sidelines on that cool Texas afternoon and began to reflect on how we don't know from day to day what life may bring.

It was over thirty years ago on a hot, summer morning on a football field in Dayton, Tennessee, that I asked someone, "Who is that guy?" I have since found out who he really is. He is an old wounded soldier. He has been through many battles and carries the scars of combat. Physically, cancer has taken its toll and left its scars, yet in him still beats the heart of a warrior. There is still that passion that drives him to fight the good fight. If Ted was not real and if Ted was trying to fight this fight in his own strength, then he would have quit a long time ago. There's the answer to being real. It's not based on our ability; it's having the supernatural power of God, his Spirit, living in us. Being real also brings hope. When I talk to Ted, I am encouraged because he is filled with hope. He knows where he is going. He and I sat in a coffee shop about a year ago just outside Atlanta and talked about heaven. He had a twinkle in his eye and expectancy in his voice when he talked about that place. I left that meeting with an extra skip in my step, thinking about the reality and glory of the ultimate consummation of the Christian life. Ted, I can openly and unashamedly say, "I love you my brother." I am thankful I have had the opportunity to see real Christianity lived out in this life. Be real. There is no other way to have true satisfaction and contentment in this life and the life to come.

Well, I could literally go on and fill another 250 pages of more of the same. I think this is enough to "wet your whistle." I believe in coaching. When you consider the influence and satisfaction and challenge of every day, you have to believe our role is not only critical, but also the most fun job on the planet! As we move on to the next chapter of the book, I hope you have been motivated to build your coaching philosophy on love, laughter, loyalty, and leadership. Be a mentor to every player. Be an example to every player. Be the most prepared coach in your league. And most of all, believe in your boys. Each one will have the potential to change the world, each one will need you, and in the end, you will be surrounded a thousand times over with great love. And may you one day be laid to rest with your whistle around your neck!

CONFLICT MANAGEMENT

Sounds so official and so tactical. It sounds tidy and neat with a hardy dose of professionalism mixed into the batter. But let me be first to tell you that after thirty years in the trenches, I have found the conflict to be anything but manageable. In fact, I have learned, as have hundreds and hundreds of former Christian school coaches, a little leaven leavens the whole lump. All it takes is one bad administrator to undermine the impact of the entire athletic department. I have considered it to be epidemic, and the proof is in the stunning numbers. Thirty years ago, right? And do you know how many of those male and female coaches are still coaching in Christian education today that started with me in 1980? Keep in mind that I have been involved in Christian education intimately in eight states, I have known coaches at over 500 schools, and I can only think of four men still standing after these many years. That's all! The male coach in a Christian school proves with overwhelming evidence that there is a great gulf fixed between their fraternity and the sometimes skewed species of holy headmasters. Oh, I know, I shouldn't point the finger. But it is what it is. Phil Farver, Terry Terrill, Mike Hall, and my brother-in-law, Steve Lykins, are the only guys still coaching in Christian education that I know of who began when I did during the Reagan Administration. Four! And three of these four have moved several times in order to find themselves the healthy environment and philosophical support necessary to provide their student/athletes an opportunity to reach their full potential and the athletic department treated as a high priority. My old buddy Terry Terrill ("Bird") is the lone exception to the rule. He started at Riverdale Baptist, and he continues to be the head baseball coach today. He has the longest tenure of any Christian school coach in America having been a Crusader for over thirty-five years. One-of-a-kind.

Four coaches. That is an insane number to me. In actual percentages, there has been a 90 percent turnover every ten years nationwide among Christian school coaches. There is no such thing as stability in Christian school athletics. It just doesn't exist. Here are some of the reasons for such chaos and then I will share my struggles, my survival, and my strategies for winning nine championships in what was many times a very toxic environment.

1. Reason #1

    An administrator who never participated in sports and sees it at best as a necessary evil.

2. Reason #2

    An administrator who feels football especially will attract the wrong type of young man (aggressive and maverick).

3. Reason #3

    An administrator who budgets more monies for elementary music than doing some outside the box efforts to subsidize athletics. The budget and stipends are anemic.

4. Reason #4

    An administrator who is intimidated by having a coach or coaches who because of their relationship with the kids are highly popular and with that comes a real ability to influence parents and teachers.

5. Reason #5

Just a good old-fashioned personality conflict between the administrator and the head coach.

6. Reason #6

Here is the one where we will find the most leaven in our lump. It brought such hardship to healthy communication and unity, which was so necessary to honor the chain of command. Unfortunately, I faced off with more than one headmaster during my career who fit this profile. The situation, when you shine the light of truth on it, will expose an administrator who makes decisions based on what will be safe for him, with no desire to work together with anyone because of leadership insecurity, which, when it manifests itself as the problem, is always the beginning of the end for a guy like me. Because you see, my whole focus and desire is always doing what is in the best interest of the kids. The minute I discovered that the headmaster was either jealous of my popularity or more focused in advancing his own interests rather than promoting the best interest of our students, I lost all respect and it began to show in my attitude.

My thirty years in Christian schools was one wild ride. I worked for some very mediocre individuals, and I worked for some of the very best of men. I do want to say that during my career, I worked for three or four different administrators who were absolutely terrific leaders and educators that gave me the support I needed in order to have the impact on the boys that would last a lifetime. And then there's the other side of the coin, where I was in a situation that was filled with conflict and turmoil due to any number of the six reasons I've already listed, and man, can I tell you it can absolutely wear you down, wear you out, and send you packing. I found it to be very frustrating through the years to develop a real love for the boys, the school community, and the church, but have one individual that could wreak havoc and undermined all your efforts. There is no doubt in my mind it is this scenario that creates such instability for coaches in Christian education. But for me, the most negative aspect of such conflicts is the toll it takes on the student body and the opportunities to build a happy environment associated with living the Christian life. The pattern always creates a dark cloud over the school and the students are conditioned to interpret the Christian life as a lifestyle of don'ts. There is an overriding legalistic approach and strategy where it seems every opportunity to grab hold of that life and life more abundant is substituted with no, no, and more no's. And sadly, the end result of our students' Christian school experience ends with their rejecting a surrendered life to Christ and a bitter taste in their mouth for the school and all but severing ties once they get that diploma in their hand. That is the real casualty of Christian education.

Sadly, the trend continues today. Watch over the course of the next few years in your local Christian school network—the coaching turnover will be significant. And if the truth be told, you can bet the house that the most influential person in the life of every athlete is going to be that coach that is leaving for greener grass.

The remedy involves making sure there is a school board or pastor who will charge the administrator to be an advocate for the coaches and allow them to create an environment of excellence and school spirit. I've actually worked under a headmaster who would not allow our varsity football team to wear their game jerseys to school on Fridays. Sometimes, the kids are more important than the rules.

These nearly thirty years I have had the most blessed opportunity to have the friendship and trust of thousands of parents. Yes, again there is the occasional nut job, but most prove to be loyal and loving friends. There were a couple of things that I always made sure the parent community knew and could depend on even if they did not agree with my choices; they knew my motives and my commitment were genuine. I always focused on finding their honey hole and what I felt to be most fair and most just for the athletes under my care. At the top of the list of consistent interaction between me and a player was to always find the best way to communicate and connect with each individual player, and that meant treating them all quite differently. No two players are exactly alike, and to treat every player exactly the same would be a very ineffective means by which to reach those players and move them from boys to young men.

So you want to know a story or two about the occasional nut job? I thought you might. Let's go all the way back to my first year in Newnan, Georgia. I was in my classroom one day midseason (just after school) when one of our dads walked in unannounced. Without any introduction, he just opened up a can of verbal you know what! He was berating me and getting louder and louder. Spit was flying across the room. He could not believe his son was an offensive guard rather than our starting quarterback. To add to the drama, this dude was a pastor (very small church). Finally, he did the one thing that he should not have done to a twenty-three-year-old, 6'0", 250 lbs. prideful man, he took off his tie, untucked his shirt, and from there, I went blank. Within a second or two, I had him pinned against the wall with his feet literally dangling above the floor. When I finally let him breathe, he stumbled out the door (leaving his tie), never to speak to me again. His son remained at guard.

Another time, there was a parent who paid a tabloid writer to attack me with accusations of illegal recruiting. The state association had a hearing on the matter, and I was cleared of any individual wrongdoing. I look back on it today and actually learned a few valuable lessons from the fireworks. Here is one that will hold true in every private/Christian school in every state: if you build a dynasty, illegal recruiting will be rumored every season of your success. There will always be mediocre coaches out there who can't and won't admit that you beat them because you're just better, and the better coaches attract the better players! So the competition needs an excuse so they play the recruiting card. I played in fourteen championship games through the years, I can't remember one single year that I wasn't rumored to cheat, except for the year our pastor had an affair, was paraded all over national television and we had a mass exodus that left us playing six-man football and a 2-8 record. Guess what? Exactly, no accusations whatsoever. My advice to you young gunslingers, regardless of the sport, ignore those voices of false accusations; I will admit I like it when people can't stop talking about my program. It all adds to the mystique.

There are several key elements to what I refer to as legally recruiting athletes. Obviously, most state associations frown on the recruitment of athletes from one school to another. There is always the issue of false addresses in the public schools as well as tuition payments made under the table in the private academies; these are the two most obvious violations at the prep level. So in order to play by the rules, it is important to steer away from any discussions of money or housing when meeting with parents of potential transfers. But I have always found that my parents make the very best recruiting coordinators for our program. And the beautiful thing about your parents selling the program is its perfectly legal. The very best way to sell your program is by word-of-mouth by satisfied customers.

Here are some elements that will make or break your success in terms of attracting high-quality athletes. First and foremost, one thing that you can always expect from me and my program is that I'm going to play the best eleven. It does not matter which booster gives the most amount of money, it doesn't matter whose parents invite me over for dinner, it doesn't matter who I sit next to at church, and it doesn't matter how good Dad thinks his son is. What matters above all else is who do I think is the very best player at each position. I have never deviated from that formula, and I've learned I will win more games with the best eleven players always on the field. Now I would add this caveat in terms of players having an opportunity to try out for the position of their choice above and beyond my initial choice. I have known many that came into our program, hoping to be the starting fullback, and it only seemed fair and reasonable for me to allow that athlete a chance to play the position that he would like to play above what might be his best position for the team. Occasionally, a coach will get pleasantly surprised. This has been the case probably a half dozen times for me through the years. It does not hurt to allow your players a chance to play a position of their liking. So if it doesn't work out, he's able to move on and assume the role that will best benefit our team and with a good attitude, having been given a fair shot at his desired spot.

Another very important area is promoting your sophomores, juniors, and seniors to college coaches. I took great pride from year one until I retired at being tireless and relentless in trying to find a place for every single player to move on and play collegiately. Through the years, we have been successful at seeing our former players go on to play not only on Saturday afternoons, but also on Sundays! I made sure that every single player who wanted to play college football got my very best effort. I would send off video, I would write letters, I would make phone calls, send e-mails, and work endlessly on highlight video to mail around the globe. I had a reputation for being able to develop players into college recruits, and everyone knew that I was at the top of the list of high school coaches who would promote their players until we found their perfect match.

Grades. If a coach really loves a player, really has a vested interest in a young man, he will take a weekly interest in checking those grades and holding athletes responsible for giving their best effort in every classroom and every subject. Every single player had to bring me a weekly grade sheet on Mondays before practice that indicated to me how they had done during the last week in each individual class as well as their cumulative average.

Another very important element in attracting athletes with real potential was the off-season program. I thought it was so very important for our weight program to reflect our interest in helping each player reach their full potential, giving them all the bells and whistles to get it done. When a young man walked in our weight room and his first impression was "wow," it sure gave us the upper hand in selling the program. I made it my personal business to be an expert in all areas of off-season training. We not only lifted hard, we did plyos, mat drills, speed work, flexibility routines, and more. Lastly, I always felt it important to encourage our players to play a second sport. This not only kept our athletes in shape, it promoted a very healthy working relationship with the entire athletic department.

We did things with a real commitment to excellence, and I had a very genuine love for each and every player, and we won consistently, but that will not make you immune to parental criticism or what will always be a very fickle fan base.

I had thought about this chapter ending with my previous paragraph. But there just isn't any way around this last point of view. I will tell you right now that I am in the minority when it comes to this subject matter. I believe that winning is the most important thing. If you were to survey Christian school administrators, athletic directors, and head coaches of all the sports we offer at the high school level, you would find a vast majority would put *giving your best effort* ahead of winning as the goal or priority of competition. Not me.

I believe that winning teaches so much more character development than losing does. The old adage, "It's not whether you win or lose that counts, its how you play the game." I think the only person who has time to sit and swallow that dumbed-down philosophy is indeed the guy who finishes second. I have found it to be much easier to have ministry, and I mean impact that changes lives, when we win. For you see, in order to win, you have to go the extra mile in the area of hard work, dedication, mental toughness, sacrifice, selflessness, and courage and commit yourself to all these character qualities at a very high level and in a very consistent daily focus. From a biblical perspective, it is very clear that every athletic contest should be played to win. Paul made it clear in 1 Cor. 9:24–27 that there is only first place that receives the victor's crown, and we as Christians should run, jump, sprint, shoot, throw better than anyone else. Winning has a unique way of building team unity and love among team members. There was a lesson I learned while playing linebacker at Maranatha Baptist Bible College. We were a very unique college football team. What set us apart was after each game, we would all grab from the sidelines gospel tracts with a sports emphasis, and while we shook hands with our opponents, we would witness to them about receiving Jesus as their Lord and Savior, praying the sinners prayer right there on the field. And I found out that it was always much easier to share Christ with the guy I played across from all day if we won. There was this respect that was extended as a result of winning.

Now I am not saying that there is no value in losing. For there are certainly many things that I have learned as a result of a heart-wrenching loss. I suppose the greatest lesson is never give up. Who among us doesn't need that reminder from time to time? But make no mistake, young men play the game of football or the sport of their choice with one purpose and that purpose is to win. Winning is fun. Winning is biblical. For those who dream big, for those who dare the impossible, losing is never the last chapter.

The Staff

Through the years, I have had quite a variety of assistant football coaches on my staff. As I mentioned in an earlier chapter, I've been very fortunate to have a number of ex-pro's join the staff and become lifelong friends to our coaches and players alike. Two were NFL Man of the Year selections and others stood out like Lloyd Mumphord who was a part of the only undefeated (17-0) Super Bowl champions when he was a cornerback for the no-name 1972 Dolphins. Interestingly, Lloyd was the smallest player in the league at 165 lbs. He wasn't taken in the draft until the sixteenth round out of tiny Texas Southern. I'll never forget the practice back about '93. Coach Mumphord was in his late forties. Somehow, the boys talked Lloyd into racing them in a 400-meter run, which is once around the track. Let's just say Lloyd still had a little gas in the tank at near fifty-years-old. The closest player on the team to run that "dare" was over 200 yards behind old number 26. From that day forward, we never said, "Get a lap." No sir. We called it a "Lloyd!" "Let's go, boys, give me two Lloyds." Classic.

I had such great assistant coaches through the years. In fact, I'll tell you one of my secrets that has been proven over and over again under the Friday night lights. As a very young coach (twenty-three and just married), I asked Bear Bryant to tell me one thing that would help me more than anything else to sustain a winner. He quickly responded by declaring, "Coach, go get yourself a coaching staff of men who know more than you do. Cut 'em loose. Give them high praise and know the name of all their children." I have tried to stay true to that advice, taking it one extra step by learning the name of their pets too!

In the beginning, there was Jay. Jay Elliott. We met at church and then I ran into him at the local sporting goods where he was a sales rep. He was and always will be the real road warrior of the dozens and dozens of staff through the years. Let me put it this way, we started together in Dallas, went to New York, out to California, and back to Texas—only this time we ended up in Houston for five years. Jay was the same age as I was. When I met him, he simply volunteered to drive the bus and help in any area of need. It didn't take me long to see in Jay a real football man. He knew as much about Texas high school football as anyone in the Lone Star state. He was great with the kids and loyal, and I mean loyal. I hired him as part of the coaching staff. He started with receivers and never left. He was a perfect fit. I coached the quarterbacks, and together, we stayed airborne to the tune of over forty points a game over a ten-year period! We had a great run together. I love Jay Elliott as much as any man on earth. I could have no better friend. Today, he teaches and coaches in a big public school in Houston. He went back to school and finished his degree, and I will always think I had a part in his realizing his dream of becoming a football coach.

Occasionally, I'd hire a dad to help. There are two who brought something special to the success and memories of days gone by. One was Sherman Stanford. I was just hired as the new head football man at Westminster Christian Academy in Opelousas, Louisiana. The school played flag football, and I was charged with coming in and converting the thing into varsity tackle football. Sherman was the flag coach, and the team was very successful under Sherman. The rules were very strange as the snap had to travel back 12-15 yards and it was an all-passing game. Sherman was a local attorney who was just a difficult person to get along with. He was very intelligent and was known for his sarcasm and lack of tact. I stunned him one day after moving into town. I showed up on his doorstep. I asked him to serve on my staff. People thought I was nuts. But I saw something in him that bore witness with my spirit. And let me be very clear, I know it was flag football in a little Christian school league, but his deep snapper was the best I'd ever seen at any level. His receivers were fantastic, I mean, he had worked some real football magic with those kids! He proved to be a wonderful assistant coach and a great friend with a very warm heart and loyal like no other.

One other dad who made a real impact on the team was Dr. Don Carroll. Don was a local dentist, very quiet gentleman. His son was Donnie Carroll who wanted to try and kick for us. I watched as they spent every day for six months out on the field in the late afternoons, kicking extra points and field goals to the tune of over one hundred balls a day. Dad would shag while Donnie worked on his steps. I watched this duo right up until time for pre-season practices to begin. I asked Don to join our staff as the official kicking coach. The two worked magic together and in the state semifinal game that first year. Donnie was our go-to guy. We made it to the state semifinal game against a heavily favored Midland Christian Mustang team that lived up to the hype. We scored with about a minute left on the clock to tie the score at 6-6. Donnie kicked the game-winning extra point into a 30 mile an hour wind. Dad just smiled. I needed smelling salt.

I could tell another hundred stories like the two I've shared with you. I remain dearest friends with the vast majority of those who served with me in the building of young men. Did I ever have to fire an assistant coach? Yes, but not often. I actually fired a coach once, and we have remained the best of friends now for almost twenty years! I have helped him secure several head coaching positions over the years. As I think about it, I've only fired three bad seeds in thirty years, ain't too bad a record really. The key is to find a guy who loves young men, is loyal, and is willing to be the waterboy if that is the job needing done right away.

I always made it my first priority to be loyal to each man working under me. What was good for the goose.

PIGSKIN PLAYBOOK

I know there will be thousands of football junkies scouring the book in hopes of finding secrets that will gain them advantage over the enemies awaiting invasion on the gridiron. Well, here is the closest thing to the Pigskin Pentagon Papers you'll ever get. I hope our approach, our philosophy, and our organizational structure helps you win more consistently than ever before. This chapter is more of a teaser to our program than a detailed presentation. If you want the full scope of my design for winning, I am available to share with coaches in person. My clinics are marinated with spiritual truths and principles essential to changing lives through our great game.

Let's begin in the off-season. We offered a 6:00 a.m. weight room workout four days a week. Stretching, plyos, mat drills and running (conditioning) are all incorporated into our preparation on the road to the state title. How important is this aspect of the program? I very rarely missed a workout, I gave out monthly awards, and all player data was displayed on a big board in a high traffic area in the high school hallway. The goal of every player is to be the best conditioned athlete on the team, in our region, and in the nation. Our goals are that high. Relentless, focused, and nasty mean, these are character traits and attitudes we fostered all the way down through the middle school. Oh, and by the way, I have used numerous lifting programs through the years, and in the end, my first choice would be the one designed for Liberty University by nationally renowned strength coach Dave

Williams. We saw incredible improvement without plateaus. Make this the most important aspect of your program.

Here are the foundational pillars upon which we build our team above and beyond good or even great. Our goal, our passion, is perfection.

1. *Make it fun.*
2. *Team first.*
3. *Never walk on or off the field (always on the run!).*
4. *Yes, sir/No, sir (good manners and respect for all teammates)*
5. *Appealing to authority: right time, right place, and right spirit.*
6. *Expect to play with pain, never hurt (mental toughness was one of our priorities).*
7. *Practice does not make perfect. Practice makes permanent. Perfect practice makes perfect. We will execute to perfection every second of drills, skills, and from the line of scrimmage.*
8. *We all wear the same game cleats, the same socks, and no writing on towels, etc. (white only). There will be no showboats on this team.*
9. *Always win the fourth quarter. Never shortcut conditioning.*
10. *Play your most physical game every down until the whistle blows. Feet, feet, feet!*

We add team goals as well as offensive and defensive goals and create a hallway board for each. Nothing quite as motivating as knowing Susie sees the boards every day!

I know this is not possible for every school due to limited prep time by the host coach or the lack of funding, but in my final years as head coach, I raised funding to produce our own two-hour Saturday morning radio show. We interviewed players, coaches, and cheerleaders. We selected Players of the Week and gave numerous other awards. We included standings, rankings, and individual statistics. Our players loved it!

Another important philosophy from which we organize our practices is an uncompromising commitment to the fundamentals. It has been my belief for the last twenty years or so that we need to block and tackle every practice. Think about it, 95 percent of all football movement is blocking and tackling! We have very safe drills for tackling, all of which reinforce keeping your head up and establishing your head across the bow.

Flexibility, speed, balance, and explosiveness are all incorporated into our drills. I superintend as the head coach over the tempo and hustle factors of our drills. I let the coaches coach the technique (and feet) while I am very verbal with encouragement to all-out effort. We often try to create an environment of one-on-one competition.

I have always been one to believe that there is so much more character to be learned and reinforced in a young man's life through winning, not losing. Therefore, I have always put a great emphasis on winning. We do not allow excuses for failure. One of my favorite sayings has always been winners don't need excuses. Let me share a true story with you from my days of coaching basketball. I do not recommend my actions as they may get you fired in today's world.

My last year to double-dip as head football and head basketball coach was at Westminster Christian Academy in the Cajun triangle of south Louisiana. We had a pretty talented group that was a real joy to coach. We had so much fun and the love among the players afforded us great team chemistry. We made it to the state tournament in Baton Rouge. We made it to the semifinals before finally losing a real heartbreaker by one point to the eventual state champs. This was back in the day when they still played a third place game prior to the state title game. So the next morning, we played one of the teams in our state with an excellent basketball reputation. They had a monster 6'10" big man in the middle. Somehow, we found a way to pull it out with a three-point win and a very nice third place state plaque. It was the first in school history.

In the locker room after the game that day, I made a stand. The reaction was mixed, and one I look back on today and just shake my head that I did not get hung by an angry mob of parents.

I asked the boys to gather up and stay on their feet so I could look them straight into their eyes. I told them how proud I was of their commitment, trust, and accomplishments of this record-setting season. We finished third in the state and won our region. This was a special group of boys and only one senior! And then I set the bar higher than anyone was willing to even whisper at the dinner table. I said that I would not include this third place plaque (it was huge) in our trophy case. It would go into storage. "Men, I did not come here to teach you to finish third. I came here to make you champions on the court and classroom. From this moment on, we never speak of this consolation trophy or season. We hit the off-season workouts like never before. You focus your whole being on this. I had borrowed the state title trophy and had it under a towel. If you'll join me, men, then put your right hand on your heart and left hand on the prize. Pray with me."

The following season, these same young men hoisted the state championship trophy. I put my right hand on my heart and my left on the prize. We prayed. The trophy? Still sits front and center in our trophy case. I did not coach the team that next year. I hired a much better basketball man than myself. It was a wonderful year of watching the Bible truth, "We reap what we sow," as well as watching these boys take a big step toward becoming champions in life.

That following year (of our consolation finish), our football team went unbeaten, our volleyball team won the AA title (state champs), and both our boys and girls basketball teams won at record pace! However, many of the parents stayed mad at me for months. The media stayed in my hip pocket the entire next year and a half. I was always good for an interesting quote. My administrator and his happy band of board members went through gallons of Maalox during my tenure.

In order to win, there must be a consistent commitment to excellence. You'll find that champions exercise the most sacrifice, dedication, mental toughness, hard work, selflessness, and the ability to rise above challenging circumstances than those who finish back in the pack. I've been able to have a greater effect on my players through the years as a result of winning. The life axiom of input equals output applies to everything we do on and off the field or court. Even so, after every game where your boys give great effort, I might suggest a good hand slap on the hind quarters, a high five and yes, displaying your third place hardware.

Pigskin Potpourri

Here's thirty years of pigskin potpourri (a collection of the best-smelling ideas and practices).

1. *Never kick, punch, push, or grab a player; you'll never survive it.*
2. *Build up and believe in each player. He may be the next president of the United States, more importantly, your grandkids' pastor!*
3. *Our players always knew they could challenge any decision made by the coaching staff as long as they chose the right time (after practice not during practice), right place (a private area rather than grandstanding in front of others), and right spirit (your tone and the words you choose must display respect for the authority). Violate any one of Rock's rules for appealing a decision, and you forfeit the right to be heard.*
4. *Be early. I never compromise this mandate. Be early or you are late and you will pay. I'm tough when it comes to this one. Make it a habit to be early for all things, and you will find life to your advantage!*
5. *Linemen always go first through the dinner line in a restaurant.*
6. *We pick the color(s) of our cleat, and we all get the same color with no exceptions. I do not force them to all buy Nike or another brand. Each player will have his own requirements*

to securing a good fit. I leave it up to each player to handle his own business.

7. We don't paint faces. And we all wear the same color receiver gloves (if you wear them at all).
8. Once you are a starter, you may "spat" your shoes if it makes you feel faster.
9. Never sit on a helmet unless running a 26.1 mile marathon appeals to you.
10. Music is a great calmer of the nerves as well as a great motivator. We allow it on trips and before games; it must be clean lyrics.
11. We try to keep a disciplined environment in everything we do. We even run on and run off the practice and game fields in what we call the swarm. We developed the idea from the University of Iowa football team. I love Hayden Fry and copied a lot of his influence on the game.
12. Helmets: we love award decals! Creates individual incentives to rise to the top of being a playmaker.
13. The locker room will be managed by our seniors and be the crown jewel of our stadium/ athletic complex, or we run till we puke.
14. Every scheme we have at the high school level is about outnumbering the opponent's offense (at the point of attack) as well as creating angle advantage on offense.
15. Every Monday, we do a grade check. I expect every player to sit in the front of the class, take thorough notes, participate in discussions, and do his homework!
16. No hats when getting off the bus or entering a building.
17. Leave a good tip at the restaurant.
18. Exercise all of our good manners learned each week.
19. No swearing.
20. Notify me before practice if you do not feel well enough to participate. We have consequences for all missed team meetings and practices.
21. I always tried to create relay competition and fun conditioning drills (like the circle drill in the old movie Vision Quest).

22. *One of my absolute priorities is helping each player who wants to play college football find his perfect fit. I make as many calls as it takes. We spend a huge amount of time working on highlight videos, and I will even take seniors to visit colleges if needed.*
23. *I never defer the opening kick-off. We want the ball now.*
24. *I prefer young ladies as managers, much more organized and reliable.*
25. *Don't ever talk while I talk (or another coach).*
26. *Our flexibility program is designed and executed much like a choreographed musical. Another area that builds pride, unity, and discipline.*
27. *This strategy usually finds more coaches resistant than receptive. I usually added or changed twenty-five or thirty plays from week to week. We were very hard to scout and prepare for. Defensively, our philosophy was designed to penetrate, penetrate, and penetrate! The read and react philosophy in my mind reminded me of practice sessions where we had our number 2 defense holding big dummies and shields (just standing there with targets on their chests, that eliminates game simulated execution). We want the opposing offense to feel pressure every time they line up on the line of scrimmage.*
28. *Always shake hands and respond with class after a win or loss.*
29. *No swearing. No exceptions. First offense equals running until rubbing shoulders with a near-death experience. Second offense equals being dismissed from the team.*
30. *I work the media relentlessly. I want to see our kids get their time on the sports page like the big boys do.*
31. *Bonus: invite parents to be as much a part of our activities as the players.*

Why Football?

Football is a game that should only be played to win. In winning, all other by-products are experienced to their fullest and most effective intent. Football simulates war like no other team sport known to man. Yet it can breed an intense loyalty and love among its members. Such admirable qualities as dedication, selflessness, hard work, courage, discipline, self-control, sacrifice, and intelligence must be exercised as a team before winning can become a constant. It is a game that allows athletic brilliance earned passage, to esteem to the glory of legends. It is a game of collision, intensity, and even brutality. Yet football is celebration, glory, and breathtaking pageantry. In essence, football is a reflection of life; the more we experience it, the greater will become our passion.

Football can be a powerful tool in building and molding biblical principles into the life of each impressionable participant, a spiritual influence that will reach far beyond the stadium lights. Let's examine how:

1. Football is a team sport. One of the first lessons to be learned in the game of football is the concept of *big team* and little me. No one player is as important as his team. This mandates each individual assuming whatever role necessary to best promote overall team effectiveness. This involves sacrifice and self-denial. Without these two character qualities, it would be impossible to follow Christ. In Matthew 16:24, we read, "Then said Jesus unto His disciples, If any man will come after me, let him deny himself, and take up his cross, and follow me."(KJV)
2. Football is a game that demands commitment. Two-a-days, pursuit drills, agility drills, sprints, more sprints, contact drills, film review, weightlifting, injuries, and worst of all-second string. Overwhelmed by the torrid heat of August and the bone-chilling winds of November, and because of the violent nature of the game, even the most enthusiastic pursuer of pigskin prowess grows weary and worn. It takes a great extra effort, especially with all the distractions afforded high school–aged boys today, to finish and

follow through to the end with their commitments. Bear Bryant said, "A quitter never quits just once." We live in a day when situation ethics more readily reflect our society as a whole than exercising the high moral responsibility of finishing a task or keeping our word, regardless of how difficult a course can become. Football is a great mechanism for continually reinforcing the importance of seeing a very difficult and demanding task through to its completion. The apostle Paul's last testament is a great witness to the steadfastness essential to living the Christian life worthy of heavenly crowning. "For I am now ready to be offered, and the time of my departure is at hand. I have fought a good fight, I have finished my course, I have kept the faith. Henceforth there is laid up for me a crown of righteousness" (2 Timothy 4:6–8a, KJV).

3. Football is a game of mental toughness. The game of football is not a game of contact, it is a game of collision. Ninety-five percent of all movement is blocking and tackling. The general objective is to physically punish your opponent in such a manner as to execute offensive and defensive schemes, which will declare your team winner by virtue of points accumulated according to your physical dominance. Simply put, the more aggressive, the better your chances. It takes courage and mental toughness to participate in the game of football. Notice I said participate rather than be a starter. Often, it's the younger or more inexperienced player that has to muster up mental toughness as he faces the bigger and better player and endures the physical abuse on a daily basis during weekday practices. However, almost every player has to learn to play with pain. A good coach will never ask a player to learn to play hurt, but will demand he play with pain. Those who do not have the brass to play this game of *hard knocks* usually turn their interest toward the more civil soccer field. It is simply a tough game for

tough young men. Paul declared in Ephesians 6:12, "For we wrestle not against flesh and blood, but against principalities, against powers, against the rulers of the darkness of this world, against spiritual wickedness in high places." (KJV) Paul also made it clear to Timothy in 2 Timothy 3:10–15 that living for Christ in a world that continually waxes worse and worse will involve persecution and that we should be ready and mentally tough as we encounter this adversity. (Verse 12: "Yea, and all that will live godly in Christ Jesus shall suffer persecution."(KJV))

4. Football is a game of discipline. I have often bantered and preached during individual drills, "If you can't control your own body, you can't control your opponents!" Although it appears to the casual fan that football is simply a game of brawn, we as coaches realize the greatest intangible asset we can achieve in our players individually and collectively is discipline. It takes discipline to stay faithful to the rigors of an off-season weight program, it takes discipline not to jump off-sides when your opponent tries to draw you off during a critical third-down. It takes discipline to block until the whistle, to pursue the ball carrier at the proper downfield angle, to keep moving your feet when pass blocking, not to drop your head when tackling, plant properly on an out pattern, stay in your lane on a kick-off, execute a proper punt return! Every motion or action required will teach technique. It is not enough to simply practice a football concept. It must be learned and executed to perfection. For you see, practice doesn't make perfect. Practice makes permanent. *Perfect practice makes perfect.* It is not a game of Xs and Os, it is a game of strict discipline.

The Christian life demands discipline. It takes discipline for us to set time aside each day for a personal quiet time in God's word. It takes discipline to keep from watching the wrong things on television or saying something that would cause us to compromise our testimony for Christ. Discipline is essential in order for us to resist temptation and keep ourselves within the boundaries of biblical obedience. Again, Paul declares in 1 Corinthians 9:27, "But I keep under my body, and bring it into subjection."(KJV) Paul was able to be so dynamic in his influence for Christ because he realized that the tremendous importance of discipline in the life of the believer.

5. Football breeds winners. It is essential for a football program to be biblical, that winning be a top priority. "It's not whether you win or lose that counts, it's how you play the game." This sounds admirable, yet nothing could be further from the truth! Our government must have coined that particular phrase, for dating all the way back to the Korean conflict, our government has had a *no-win* policy. It was a great feeling of national pride when Stormin' Norman was clearly given authority to win! We need to use football as a tool to breed winners; we should envelop our entire approach to a philosophy of win, win, win. Paul makes it very clear in his letter to the church at Corinth that we all run in a race. He is speaking here of a spiritual race, but he refers to the ancient Olympics when he states "only one receive the prize." That, of course, was the exact protocol involved in awarding the event champion with a ceremonial winner's wreath. There was no awarding of his silver or bronze medal! Paul, after pointing out that only one competitor can be the winner, concludes by very clearly admonishing the believers, "So run that ye may obtain." In other words, we should strive to be first in all that we do. It is not a vain precept, but rather a biblical command! Winning is important. Football can be a great laboratory in developing winners for Christ!

6. Football builds self-esteem. Something magical happens to a young man when he dons the uniform of the home

team on a clear September Friday night. There is a sense of pride, belonging, accomplishments, and even a small measure of independence. Many young men today look to their coach as a surrogate father. They come from broken or dysfunctional homes. Their self-image is very low and insecurity permeates their entire thought process. Because football is so much like war, there is a special bonding that takes place between coach and player. The very nature of the game breeds genuineness, camaraderie, and a heart-felt love for one another. This very wonderful game can provide the opportunity to give a young man a pat on the back that could very possibly change his life. As coaches, we should never forget that football provides a tremendous opportunity to "Let nothing be done through strife or vainglory, but in lowliness of mind let each esteem others better that are than themselves. Look not every man on his own things, but every man also on the things of others. Let this mind be in you, which was also in Christ Jesus" (Philippians 2:3–5, KJV)).

7. Football is a great tool for building leaders. Each army must have an effective chain of command. There is the platoon sergeant who gives the critical command to fire while his platoon lays motionless behind enemy lines. There must be the lieutenant who surveys the results and reports his findings all the way up the strategic command to the five-star general. Leadership is critical to the success or failure of any organization or united effort. The successful football coach is one who leads by example. A dynamic leader will breed or compel others to leadership roles. Paul Brown so influenced others to leadership that eleven Super Bowls have been won by his former assistant coaches. Paul "Bear" Bryant compelled so many players into leadership positions that it is staggering the way he has influenced college football. Today's most successful college coaches are

a vast majority of ex-Bryant players. His greatest legacy is the number of once timid freshman who, through Bryant's influence, grew to mature into great leaders and role models for the last two generations. Football certainly affords opportunity to develop leadership in our young men. It is a game for those who can think clearly under pressure, to take the opportunity to step forward under healthy guidance and direction from the coaching staff. Captains can be given certain responsibilities that have helped develop leadership as well as contribute to the actual success of the overall game plan. Starters can be motivated to leadership by their elevated status among their classmates. They can also be given leadership roles in helping to develop second-team players at their respective positions. Eventually, through the influence of football, might many of our young men be found in leadership capacities as those mentioned in Hebrews 13:7, "Remember them which have the rule over you, which has spoken unto you the word of God, whose faith follow, considering the end of their conversation." (KJV)

8. Football is practical. Yes, indeed, football is a very practical sport. This means that players will have to commit a couple hours a day, usually four days a week to the summer conditioning/weight training program. Football becomes a very practical means by which to keep kids occupied (and tired) during a period when often too much free time can lead to trouble and tragedy. The anticipation of actual game competition begins with the first week of the new school year, how practical! It does not take a rocket scientist to realize that in order to participate in these Friday night games, one is required Monday through Thursday night to study! Players may still only consider school work a necessary evil, but what a great opportunity to get them off on the right cleat. As I said, very practical. Football teaches in young

men a strong work ethic. Again, we're back to why winning must be emphasized. Here is a great opportunity to teach a long-lasting object lesson that hard work equals success, which is well worth the travail, tears, and time. It reinforces the five Ps: proper planning prevents poor performance, positively practical!

9. Football is fun. One of the fondest memories I have of my childhood is that of football. From the time I was eight years old, it was always great fun to assemble the neighborhood gang together and play a spirited game of touch or even tackle football. Then came the splendor of my high school years. What could be more fun than scoring the winning touchdown, state championship rings, sacking the quarterback, returning a kick off all the way, preserving the win with an acrobatic interception in the end zone, winning in over time, the awards banquet, the emotional pregame speech, pep rallies, enemy paint on your helmet, a great chop block, the traditional birthday letterman's jacket, a proud hug from Dad after the game, successfully stopping the opposition on fourth and inches, game uniforms with black gloves, the Sunday morning newspaper photo, a college questionnaire, post-game pizza with Patty Sue, the roar of a packed bleachers, the coin toss, homecoming hayrides, and memories of football and fun that will last a lifetime.

10. Big man on campus! Stats prove the best basketball players, baseball players, track stars, and wrestlers are the young men who play football in the fall. Football is a great way to start the school year and stay conditioned, flexible, and confident when heading into that second season.

*** The following packet is a sample of one of my pre-season regulations and expectations. I've included it for you to use as a reference if you so desire.

Fighting Saints Football 2006

Welcome to the family! Summit football is about believing in the power of God within you and belonging to something that offers unconditional love. Believe/belong. This is our theme for our inaugural season of fighting Saints football.

The 2006 season will be a varsity program. It will be for all young men entering eighth through eleventh grade. We will not have a senior class. However in the spring of 2007, we will step up into the FHSAA Class A varsity ranks with a full roster of ninth through twelfth grade letterman!

There are several prerequisites to participation on the varsity team this fall; it begins with a commitment to our summer program.

1. Each player will have the opportunity to participate in thirty summer lifting sessions. You must commit to twenty-five sessions if you are already a student at Summit Christian school. Family vacations are encouraged as well as church and sports camps. These absences are excused. Workouts will be Monday through Thursday from 4:00 to 6:00 p.m.
2. Official practice begins on July 31 and is mandatory. The week of July 31 through August 5 will be our week of two days. Again, mandatory! We will practice on campus from 9:00 a.m. till 11:30 a.m. and again from 6:00 p.m. to 8:30 p.m. The first three days we will be in shorts and helmets only. Thursday through Saturday, we will be in full pads.
3. Physicals must to be completed and on file in my office before the Miami football camp or the first day of practice on July 31.
4. Each player and one parent must sign the player/parent contract before participation in preseason practice on July 31.

5. Cost per player will include a $200 athletic fee, $75 for the game jersey, $75 for in cleats, a $25 spirit pack for summer and in season practices (shorts and T-shirt), and $15 ortho mouthpiece.
6. We will be making at least one two-day trip (Munroe Day School in Quincy) during this season, which will require additional funds for housing and food.
7. Each player is expected to give his very best effort in the classroom. Each Monday, every player will be required to have a grade check form completed, signed by each teacher, and personally handed to me for review. I expect each player to have a commitment to excellence on the field, in the classroom, and all school relationships. Our goal this year will be an overall team GPA of 3.0. Each player will be expected to be a positive leader on campus and an example of great character and kindness.
8. Each player is encouraged to enroll in a weight training elective during the school day. Very important. This will allow each athlete to reach his full physical potential and at the same time allow him to participate in at least one other team sport during the school year. I strongly encourage each player to play at least one more sport as this will only help him become a better man and football player. I've had over 180 former players go on to play football on the collegiate level, 85 percent participated in at least one other sport for two or more years. Do it!

Lastly, it is not my intention to build a program that operates in the shadows of Kings Academy, Glades Day, Benjamin, or North Florida Christian. It is my expressed purpose to build a program that conquers these formidable foes. They have facilities, tradition, and a recognizable place in the winner's circle. I have your son, you, and a calling of God. That is enough. Please lock arms with me by joining the sports committee tonight. And then, believe and belong and buckle your seat belt!

Player/Parent Contract 2006

Each player is expected to be open to the message of the good news of Jesus Christ.

Each player is expected to be punctual for all summer workouts and season practices unless prior approval is given by the head coach.

Unexcused tardies to workouts/practices will result in extra running after practice

One unexcused practice will result in one missed game.

Two unexcused practices will result in dismissal from the team.

Respect at all times to all who believe and belong!

Team first.

Never walk. Always on the run.

Yes, sir/no, sir.

Please/thank you.

Appeal = right time, right place, and right spirit.

No hats in buildings.

No cleats in buildings.

No trash ever on the locker room floor.

Tennis shoes and cleats always.

Football attire is required for all workouts and practices: T-shirts, shorts, tennis shoes, cleats, no jewelry, no boots.

Players are expected to be an example every time they are in their car on the property of how to comply by the five mile-per-hour speed limit. Reserve your speed for sprints.

No player is ever allowed in the training room without supervision of the trainer or coach.

No player is allowed to touch a first aid kit, coaches and training staff only.

Report all injuries. Do not treat yourself.

Keep all practice gear washed as needed.

Turn in all game uniforms immediately following each game.

Only your spirit pack T-shirt may be worn under your game jersey.

Game jerseys may only be worn on game day.

Team curfew on the night before a game is 10:00 p.m.

Never sit on a helmet. Take a knee (our official resting position).

An unsportsmanlike conduct penalty will result in a one-game suspension. Never let this happen.

Every player is required to ride the team bus to every game. Players may ride home with parents if prior approval is given by the head coach.

Never talk while a coach is talking. Never.

Summer and preseason practice suggestions:

1. Each player should eat a light breakfast without milk.
2. Each player should bring a cooler filled with good old-fashioned water or sports drink of choice.
3. Lots of rest, sleep, and weekend recovery running.
4. No Cokes, no sugar, and no grease!

Each player and parent needs to carefully read the parent student handbook and make themselves aware of all the discipline policies set forth by the school disciplinary administration. This handbook will be the final authority of all matters of discipline. Detentions will be considered unexcused tardies. Suspensions will result in unexcused absences.

I, _____, fully understand each rule and responsibility set forth by the football and athletic department and do fully commit to cooperating to the best of my ability to each one. I will do my best to be a Christian example in the halls as well as the athletic field as I represent the Fighting Saints football program and my family. I intended to finish the entire year and understand quitting is not an option unless prevented from participation due to an injury or poor health. I believe and belong.

_____   _____

Signature of Player   Date

We pledge full support to the Fighting Saints football program and the rules set forth in this document. We will do our best to be an active member of the sports committee for the 2006–2007 school year.

_____   _____

Signature of Parent   Date

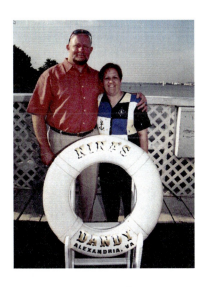

The single most important ingredient to a successful coaching career is a spouse that is completely committed to being a full partner in your dreams and goals. I married the best coach's wife on the planet. She is my biggest fan, she has never once complained about my time away from home, managed five children by herself, cooked meals for more players than McDonald's has sold Happy Meals.

Family photo with all five kids at Kelsey's wedding, the highest rated episode ever on "Say Yes to the Dress Atlanta!"

Brooks Bellows at the state championship ring ceremony at Westminster. He played at a whooping 130 lbs.! He loved the game and loved his coach. Brooks holds two distinctions: the smallest athlete to ever play for me and the hardest working player I ever coached. He was buried in his game jersey.

Here are Nolan and Gayle Simmons. One day, they asked me to come out to their lodge. Mr. Simmons said, "Coach, you changed the direction of my son's life, so I want to help you change the direction of your football program." He handed me a check for $125,000.

Teddy, made First Team State as a wide receiver.

Nile rushed for 2,200 yards his senior year along with 33 touchdowns. He fell less than 100 yards short of Herschel Walker's rushing record.

Jimmy Johnson, head coach of the Miami Hurricane, came calling one day hoping to recruit Diego London (middle) meeting in my office. Diego signed with the 'Canes, won three national championship rings, and went on to play in the CFL.

Coach Rock in his holy of holies.

Morgan Academy 37, Meadowview 13. Both schools are located in Selma, Alabama. It was our first win over Meadowview in many years. They were the defending state champs.

MARK TIDWELL, left, won awards for football defensive MVP, football MVP, basketball MVP, Newnan Times-Herald MVP and the 1980-81 Coaches' Trophy. Coach Ted Knapp is shown with Tidwell.

Here is Mark Tidwell and a first year coach at our 1980–81 athletic banquet. Mark cleaned up that night. He passed away from a long battle with cancer. This book is dedicated in his memory.

Jason Burns represents my entire ministry. A great player, transfers in to play for us, I lead him to Christ, had a stellar college career, came back to coach with me. He was my defensive coordinator for six years. I love him like I do my own boys.

Westminster 29, Southern Lab 13. This was the biggest upset of the season according to media from Baton Rouge to Lake Charles. We literally stunned the Cajun country of South Louisiana.

Mike Kershaw, best player I ever coached. He went on to lead Delta State to a Southland Conference championship at 160 lbs.

Kris Kershaw. He was heavily considered as the best player I ever coached. Went 13-0 as my quarterback in California, threw 33 TD passes, and was voted the First Team All-State Quarterback.

Here are the Four Horsemen of Riverdale (L to R) Jason Burns #55/ Craig Lewis #2/ Scott Torregrossa #7/ Diego London #99. Scott Torregrossa is simply the absolute best athlete I ever coached. Incredible football, basketball, baseball, track (10.6 100m), high jump (vertical jump of 40 inches).

The Fantastic Five from Westminster. (L to R) Shelton Jordan, Joel Comeaux, Mike Kershaw, Alex Schermann, Reggie Richard, all headed to college on a football scholarship. Four of the five were only in their second year of playing football.

Coach Knapp receiving the California championship trophy. The school CEO called Knapp "the best football coach in America" in the post game celebration.

The old linebacker speaking to several hundred area football coaches. His speeches captivate all ages.

ROCK REFLECTS

*T**his has been a real blast. I love connecting with so many of you all around the US and Canada. I hope our true stories have inspired you to scoop up your own five smooth stones and run straight for the Goliaths in your life. No fear! With Christ as your strength, the victory is already won! The purpose behind these devotional studies and testimonies is to inspire you to go deeper in your own relationships, especially the one with Jesus Christ. I hope we have struck the right cord between living life with more passion and that of setting your sail to risk the rapids. I guess the major call of these pages is to stretch yourself by dreaming your biggest dream and with Christ at your side, conquering new challenges far beyond your normal reach. Secondly, I hope you have been able to see the unspeakable joy of pouring yourself into others with unconditional love going so much deeper than words. The most satisfying and full life comes from serving others in both word and deed.*

I'm a big fan of Jim Valvano. He has inspired thousands upon thousands of cancer patients to fight the good fight. His coaching style was similar to mine, a player's coach. He passed on, leaving quite a legacy and with undeniable courage and dignity. However, we might not totally agree in terms of how much cancer can and does infiltrate our lives. I have found it to be quite the thief. In my case, it has taken a great deal from me. I am not the man I once was. The fact is that I have had to retire from most activities, almost all leadership positions and opening my own jar of jelly (my thirteen-year-old daughter handles opening most cans and jars for me as well as stubborn doorknobs) as I have had to surrender to being somewhat put out to pasture. I've gone from Superman to Jimmy Olsen. I am not the sharp and commanding speaker I once was. I struggle to find words, and due to short-term memory loss (chemo), it takes others to help me remember details from just a week ago. I have no energy most of the time and just walking out to get the mail is a challenge. I can no longer run or even jog. I cannot jump off the ground and my balance is atrocious (I fall two or three times a week). My depth perception is quite skewed due to losing the sight in my left eye. I struggle reaching for things as well as stepping up or down stairs. Taking a shower just about requires the same amount of training and effort as if I were an Olympic decathlete. I've lost all feeling in my feet and toes, I have carpal tunnel disease in each thumb and palm, I've lost a good bit of hearing in both ears, my singing voice sounds more like a steam engine, my plumbing is rusting and giving me problems every single day (and night), and I have lost most of my ability to rest (sleep). I get maybe 2-2 ½ hours a night. My sons must now live with the fact that neither was ever able to beat Dad one on one in basketball (no more rematches). My immune system is completely compromised due to chemo. In the last two years, I've almost died from shingles (five days in ICU) and pneumonia (which resulted in an eleven-day stay in ICU, four of those days on a ventilator). Throw in a few daily surprise aches and pains along with two terminal diseases and dialysis, well, you begin to get the picture. God is right there with me. He tells me I've slowed down some, but to rejoice because I'm still vertical! True dat!

    I can tell you the thing I miss the most is my ability to coach football. I miss the smell of the gridiron, the sounds of young men in combat on the line of scrimmage, the beat of the drum line, the cheering crowd, the National Anthem, my always impassioned pregame speeches, the smell of grills at the concession stand, the cleats clanging on the asphalt, preparing all week in the film room for the next opponent, and yes, our daily devotions together as a team family. Most of all, I miss the boys. I miss them so much. Cancer has robbed me of the one thing I did well in life: coach. Not too terribly long ago, one of my players (three-year starter) told me that the day I walked into his life with my whistle around my neck was the day he no longer thought about putting a rope around his. Those moments change you both.

Thank God for memories. I have enough gridiron graffiti in my mind's eye to keep me celebrating life and relationships for all my remaining days. I see God in it all. And the most amazing truth of all? Neither time nor distance or cancer can ever dull the love we have for each other. I was so blessed to live as a coach. Now, with a whistle around my neck, I will get to die as one. I'm fifty-seven years old at the time of this writing, which means I have "boys" now turning fifty too. And you know what I love as much as anything after all these years? Even those fellows who are now grandparents introduce me to their families as "Coach." I was, I am, and always will be "Coach." Oh, thank you, God. I wear my title knowing it was the highest of callings and the best of days!

One final story, one I must share. It is the story about my last season pacing the sidelines as a head coach (Sherwood Christian Academy). As I look back on it, I can only attribute the six-month experience to God's grace and goodness.

There were whispers all around our school offices and hallways about me stepping down (seems my diagnosis at the Mayo Clinic of estimating less than a year to live spread like a wildfire at school, the Albany area, and with several thousand friends across the country). I, of course, rejected the medical prognosis and looked to God to give me one more year. I won't tell you it was easy or pain free; it wasn't. However, I hid my physical struggles as effectively as any Oscar-nominated actor. Well, almost as well. There was one game where we were on the road and playing a region perennial power. We jumped out on them quickly. Late in the second quarter, we were up 19-0 and in total control on both sides of the line of scrimmage. Then it happened: I passed out right there on the sideline in front of God and country (about 2,500 hundred fans). I had just been going too hard in addition to three times a week of four-hour infusions of chemotherapy.

I was somewhere near sixty pills a day too. Anyway, I was carted off in an ambulance while our kids seemed a little out of sync and my episode sure knocked the wind out of them. Final score was Tift Area, 42, Sherwood, 19. Ouch.

Besides the Tift Area fiasco, we had the best season in the twenty-three-year history of the football program. It was our first winning record ever, and we even made the playoffs! I was voted the Albany Herald Coach of the Year and my junior son rushed for over 1,200 yards (he ended his career with over 6,000 rushing yards and 87 touchdowns). To this day, I remain in awe of God giving me the strength to have that last year with my boys, my son, and my whistle.

I suppose I couldn't be blamed for shutting down in terms of hearing those words at Mayo, "Coach, you're terminal and the morbidity rate for your parallel diseases is eleven months." But if there is anything I want you to take away from the book it is this: as we arrived back home the day of my diagnosis, I walked upstairs to our bedroom and was alone for the first time since hearing I had cancer and it was going to take my life. I stood looking out the bedroom window into our back pasture and I began talking aloud to God. It went something like this, "Well, God, I guess this isn't a surprise to you. In fact, now that I think about it, it seems obvious that you have allowed this cancer into my life. And I guess if you allowed it, then you must have purpose in it, and I feel compelled right now to tell you I will not focus my thoughts, prayers, or daily living on being healed of cancer. Since you allowed it, which means it has purpose, then I just want to live out my last days totally focused on being found faithful to those purposes." I have not wavered from that resolve. I want God to smile on me as I stand before his throne and hear those words, "Well done, Ted, you are a good and faithful servant."

It's quite supernatural (in other words, God has the steering wheel!) to be diagnosed with a terminal disease, and yet I'm here this morning at 4:30, rejoicing in the Lord, full of a peace that passes all understanding and a joy unspeakable! How can this be, one might ask? Well, let me take it one more step. What is the greatest demonstra-

tion of love? That's easy, trust! The marriages that last a lifetime are firmly built on trust above all other attributes or acts. So if I (or you) really love God, then it will be quite easy to put all my trust in my Sovereign, omniscient, omnipresent, immutable, eternal, merciful, one and only God! I rest in him. I trust him.

I believe to love God with all our heart is best captured in the book of Job. Having lost everything, including his entire family, his wealth, and his health, what was the immediate response of this man of God? In spite of all his friends demanding he curse God and die, he speaks one of the most poignant expressions of all Scripture, "Though He slay me yet will I trust Him." (Job 3:15, KJV) I sit here now, dear friends, and the tears just fall. I want for all my brothers and sisters to share in this great truth with me. What hope I have in Jesus! I do not care if I am healed or if I must suffer. I trust him though he slay me. If the rest of my journey is walking through the valley of death (in pain and suffering), I fear not for I know Jesus will be there to provide the strength, courage, and peace needed to die with dignity and to "Leave a Mark" for my children that death has no sting. Jesus won my victory with his death on the cross and his glorious resurrection! I'll see the band of angels comin' after me, and then in the blink of an eye, I'll see Almighty God on his throne and he will welcome me something like this, "Welcome home, Coach. Let's trade that old whistle for a new crown!"

As you may have noticed, I did not ask any moms or ladies to be contributors to this project. Let me assure you, I could have included scores of the opposite gender as they out-hustled their counterparts many times over and were the backbone of every booster club stop and/or fund-raiser along the way, albeit content to be in the background. But it would be an incredible omission and injustice to not ask my wife to share with you her thirty-year journey as a coach's wife and, more importantly, these last five years as a caregiver (and Mom, assistant coach, Grammy, full-time employee, church member, handy man, taxi, dog groomer, housekeeper, cook, lawn care person, and the official Bank of Knappville).

I will tell you this (and every person who has ever known Shari will tell you without hesitation): my wife has been the gold standard of what a coach's wife should be. She has cooked for hundreds and hundreds of players and coaches and attended every single game I've coached unless she was delivering one of our five children or having emergency gall bladder surgery. She has gone the extra mile a thousand times over as my partner in this labor of love. There were times I was ready to walk away from my calling, but Shari's cool head, encouragement, and sixth sense kept me focused on the things most important (like the boys). Her work ethic and ability to juggle ten things at once without ever complaining always seemed supernatural. Man, do I love this woman. Yes, I outpunted my coverage!

Her role changed six years ago. Without any warning, she became my twenty-four-hour nurse. She can tell you every single struggle and challenge I have had these six years of being captive to cancer; she can do it in chronological order without any hesitation. She can tell you every medication (probably a hundred or more) I have had to keep organized. She can tell you how many doses and the exact time of day they were to be taken. I never even had to know the name of my meds because Shari was so incredibly thorough. She has waited on me hand and foot, and the demands have been relentless as I have struggled walking, talking, eating, hearing, losing sight in my left eye, chronic joint pain, twenty-four surgeries, shingles, pneumonia, gross fatigue, and major body infections due to complications from dialysis. She has never once complained or allowed herself a break. One example: During my nine-day stay in ICU last year for pneumonia, my caregiver and bride left my side a total of one hour (day 4) to catch a quick shower. If they ever create a Hall of Fame for spouses, I hope I get a vote.

Shari's Contribution
(Caregiver Here)

I have always been someone's daughter, little sister, friend, employee, Mom, or Grammy, but I never thought about being a caregiver until a phone call from a doctor at Mayo in May of 2008.

I remember well the call from the nephrologist at Mayo that the results from Ted's recent kidney biopsy were back and he was diagnosed with amyloidosis, a treatable but incurable disease. I immediately called two lifelong friends for counsel on how to break it to him and our family. I hit the Internet to gather all the information I could regarding the disease and was dumbfounded at the rarity of the diagnosis and the published morbidity rate of eleven months. I composed myself and met him at the upper campus of Sherwood Christian Academy as I often did after leaving my job at Sherwood Baptist Church. We sat at a picnic table right outside the little prayer chapel on campus, and I gave him the diagnosis and all the information I had collected. He assured me that he was fine and just needed to be by himself for a while to take it all in. After several phone calls to family and friends, the news began to spread quickly. With more questions than answers at this point, we decided to take it one day at a time. This was also the beginning of our great journey of prayer, not just praying ourselves, but receiving the blessing of having thousands pray along with us for grace and guidance as we entered unknown territory.

I guess we need a little history to get us to this point. I love football; it has always been a part of my life. When we were kids in the youth league, my dad coached, my two older brothers played, I was a cheerleader, and my mom ran the concession stand out of the back of a converted milk truck. Football filled all of my fall seasons even through college days. I met Ted when he was an assistant coach at a small Bible college in Atlanta. We fell in love and were married and immediately jumped into "our" first coaching job. It was always something we did together as we felt it was "our" ministry and never just a job.

Our ministry has led us down many roads in many places. Countless faces dart through my mind even as I am writing. Everyone from pastors, administrators, teachers, assistant coaches and their families, parents, coaching buddies, and school support staffs, but most of all players. We still call them boys, although most of them are now men with careers and families. Our greatest pride and joy, outside of raising our own children and enjoying our grandchildren, have been the boys that have touched our lives in so many ways. They were always like sponges when it came to Xs and Os and could never have had a better teacher than Coach Knapp or Coach Rock that he now goes by. He was able to impart his love for the game to them on the field, and they responded with lots of wins and several championships in several states. While winning was a great feeling, our greatest satisfaction often came off the field. The countless boys (and girls) that we were able to lead to Christ were a great testimony to God's grace in our ministry. There were many, many boys who were lacking a father figure for one reason or another that clung to the leadership that Ted and his staff provided. The Lord saw fit to end our coaching career through cancer. That was not something we saw coming.

There have been too many medical this and thats to even remember during these last six years; however, I do have to recall some of them occasionally for those in the medical profession. We have learned so much on this journey through cancer. We have made countless friends along the way and have watched as the Lord used them to bless us in so many ways. We have been sustained through prayer, moral support, financial support, and lots of needed hugs along the way. Our children and grandchildren have seen an outpouring of love and respect for their earthly father and their Heavenly Father. In those tearful moments when you sometimes think you just can't handle another hurdle, the Lord provides his grace in his time. Sometimes, it comes in the form of a card in the mail, an uplifting phone call, a silly Facebook post, or even a comment from one of the grandkids followed by a much needed hug and sloppy kiss. These are the things I remember about this journey. The long days and nights during chemo, the back to back autologous stem cell transplants in Atlanta, the two stays in ICU at Emory for a total of fourteen days, and the numerous procedures and dialysis as a result of the kidney failure seem to fade when I hear our grandson saying to me on a recent family beach vacation while playing in the waves, "Grammy, this is the best day ever." Only God has the power to give us the daily grace to go on and complete the journey. Ted often says God allowed the cancer, and we only hope to be found faithful in finding the purpose for this journey. Our prayer as a couple is that all those who have been touched by our journey in one way or another see Christ and are brought into a closer relationship with him.

While I never planned to be a caregiver, I also never planned to be a writer. The real writer in our family asked me to be a part of this project even though it takes me out of my comfort zone. It has been a joy to be a coach's wife these past thirty-four years, and I plan on enjoying the next thirty as the wife of a successful author.

Rock Reflects

I have shared just the tip of the iceberg in regard to the stories from my thirty-year career. One subject we have yet to address is who is my favorite player of all time? That's a tie between Teddy Knapp and Nile Knapp (go figure)! I was very fortunate, in all seriousness, to have both boys on my teams. Teddy was a First Team All-State Receiver, and Nile rushed for more yards and touchdowns than any other player I've ever coached (6,013 yards and 87 TD's / almost identical career numbers as Hershel Walker!). You can watch him work his magic on YouTube by simply typing in "Nile Knapp senior highlights." Of course, neither one was ever the 1974 Notre Dame Club of Chicago Player of the Year (thank you very much). It will be one of the greatest joys of my life to battle the cancer long enough to see one of my grandson's play his first game of tackle football. What a day that will be!

As I leave this chapter, I want to dedicate all my memories of the game I love to the five children I love. You kids made many sacrifices through the years, including an absent dad during the season and the constant carousel of moving you from school to school. I think the first word you all learned as toddlers was "U-haul." I love you, Teddy, Katie, Kelsey, Nile, and Kirby. Always take great care of Mom once I'm gone.

I hope with all hope this book had real meaning for you. I love the game of football. It has been one of life's great treasures. I believe there will be football in heaven (read Randy Alcorn's Heaven). I've already started to prepare for my first draft. My number 1 pick will be Samson. My next pick will be David. I figure if one can bring down coliseums and the other guy can kill a lion, a bear, and a nine foot tall defensive tackle with the league leading Philistines—and do it without a helmet or shoulder pads—well, talk about a strong start for the Heavenly Hawkeyes! I'm gonna need my whistle!

In the meantime, can't wait for that first coin toss. You call it in the air.

DEVOTIONALS

The final section of the book is a compilation of devotionals suitable for coaches and athletes. Several of the devotions were written by my former players all of whom are now preaching full-time. The majority of the devotionals I wrote and would encourage you to use them for personal growth at the start of each new day. I would be happy to send you thirty new devotionals each month by simply requesting them via e-mail at: chalktalkrock@att.net.

This first devotion was submitted by David Henneke. David was my quarterback in Dallas back in the late '80s. He is the senior pastor at First Baptist Church in Independence, Kansas.

Deo Valente

> Now listen, you who say, "Today or tomorrow we will go to this city or that city, spend a year there, carry on business and make money. Why, you do not even know what will happen tomorrow. What is your life? You are a mist that appears for a little while and then vanishes."
>
> (James 4:13–14, NIV)

In this text, James warns us about the sin of presumption, and he does it in the context of using an illustration very familiar with his readers. He uses an analogy of someone, like a Jewish merchant, who makes his plans to go to another city, spend a year there buying and selling until he is ready to come back home with a profit.

This plan presumes that his plans are in fact his to make. Did you notice how God was not included in the planning process? This merchant simply made his plans for himself.

Now there is nothing wrong with making plans. In fact, Scripture is pretty clear that we should make plans and prepare before we act upon something. Planning before we act is not what this text is talking about. James is warning us not to make plans without including God in the planning process.

The point of this text is to warn those who feel completely self-sufficient, those who are perfectly at peace making their own decisions and planning their own lives. When you do this, you live with little meaningful trust placed in God.

So many believers are living their lives as though they only need God when they have an emergency.

What's the solution?

V. 15: "Instead, you ought to say, IF this is the Lord's will, we will live and do this or that." (NIV)

We must realize that life is a gift from God. In order to experience life in its fullest, as we plan, we must include God in our planning. It's not complicated. How different would our plans be if we started the decision making process by asking, "God, what do you want me to do?" and/or "Father, how do you want me to respond to this situation?"

Here's the thing. If you seek his input from the beginning, it will change everything for you.

Christians, for hundreds of years, use to write the initials DV at the end of their letters. They would sign their names; then they would write the letters DV. Those initials stood for the Latin phrase, "Deo Valente," which means "God willing."

James says that this ought to be our response to life. So how does this look in our everyday decisions? Consider this:

Have you talked to God about your retirement plans? Or have you simply presumed that you could do it whenever you wanted to?

Have you talked to God about your educational plans? Have you asked him what he thinks about your plans to pursue a degree? Or have you simply thought going back to school your decision to make?

Have you asked God his opinion on your plans to get married? Have you asked him what he thinks about your plans to file for divorce?

What about that person you are dating? I know you think that they are perfect for you, but have you considered what God thinks?

Does God want you to remain single for a while? Oh, I know that might not be what you want, but do you know what he is planning for you?

Ultimately, will you surrender your whole life to live "Deo Valente"?

Tom Jordan

This devotion is written by Pastor Tom Jordan. Tom played for me at Landmark Christian School in Montgomery, Alabama. We went 12-0 that year and finished number 1 in the country among small Christian schools. Tom is the senior pastor of Thomas Mill Baptist Church in Clanton, Alabama.

God Can Do So Much with So Little!
John 9:6–7

Here is a man with a huge problem. He is blind, wandering through life, stumbling, bumping into things, having to learn to navigate without vision. Something great happened in this man's life. He met Jesus! Like so many others that are wandering through life, they need Jesus! No matter how big your problem is, Jesus can do the miraculous! Many times over, Jesus can work a miracle with small insignificant solutions. Jesus picked up clay from off the ground and spit in the clay, as if to make a salve. This salve was very primitive, but very effective! This clay was used to solve a huge problem; the blind can now see. Our Lord shows he can do so much with so little!

I. A little statement. Genesis 1:3: "Let there be light!" (NIV) It's just four words, but what a difference they made. The earth was without form, void, and filled with darkness, just as a lost soul. One little statement, "Let there be light," and now the light pierces the darkness and God shows he can do so much with so little. Two thousand years ago, Jesus, the light of the world, pierced the sinful darkness, and the people that sat in darkness saw great light. The world was nothing, and God spoke and made something, and so also is man without God. He is nothing, but when God speaks to your heart and mine, and we hear, God can do so much with so little!

II. A little lad. John 6:9 says, "There is a lad here." Jesus says to the disciples, "Give ye them to eat." (KJV) My, how the problems begin to appear. There are five thousand men, not counting women and children. How are we going to feed them? Well, that is Jesus's command. You might say he has asked them to do the impossible. Excuses are given, and for that matter, we could say they were legitimate reasons, not just excuses. Who then will rise out of the masses to try to do God's bidding? The great Simon Peter? John the Beloved? Maybe one of the disciples or perhaps a great father and husband. No, what's this? It's a little lad with two small fish and five loaves. I have a sneaky suspicion that this little lad may have said to the Lord, "I am not much, and I don't have much, but what I have and what I am is yours!" Well, my friends, that's all it took because God can do so much with so little! Not only was the five thousand fed, but twelve baskets were left over. We also have been given an impossible task. "Go ye into all the world and preach the gospel to every creature" (Mark 16:15, KJV). I ask you who will rise out of the masses and allow God to do so much with so little?

III. A little name. Acts 13:9: "Who is also called Paul." (KJV) Saul, the name means "big"; however, Paul means "small." Paul is the name the great apostle was known by in his ministry, but before his conversion, he was known as Saul. God wanted to do something great in the life of Saul, but before the power of God could be displayed in his life, a great humbling experience had to take place and that great experience took place on the Damascus road. After God had revealed himself to Paul, Paul answered, "Lord, what wilt thou have me to do?" (Acts 9:6, KJV) Paul realized that his true position before God was very humbling. We truly are not much, but God once again shows he can do so much with so little. Paul went on to start at least sixteen churches in pagan countries and wrote fourteen books of the Bible, all this without computers, cars, phones, radios, or the printing press. Through humility, Paul was able to excel and succeed!

IV. A little faith. Matthew 17:20: "If ye had faith as a grain of mustard seed." (KJV) A mustard seed is about the size of a sesame seed, not very big at all. I was talking to a lady about her faith and inviting her to accept Christ as her personal Savior. Her reply was "I just don't have enough faith!" One of the great truths that we learn about our Lord is it does not take a lot of faith, just a little faith. Matthew 19:14 says, "Suffer little children, and forbid them not, to come unto me: for such is the kingdom of heaven." (KJV) We see many times over God can do so much with so little!

Influence
by Coach Rock

Johnson is sitting in a restaurant bragging about how he is the best fisherman in the county. Little does he know the game warden is sitting at the next table. He is going on and on, and just as he is about to pay the bill and leave, he says, "And I don't even need a rod and reel or bait! With that, the game warden said, "Johnson, you are full of hot air." Well, Johnson decides he will show this game warden, so he invites him to go fishing with him the next morning.

That morning, they meet at the lake and jump in Johnson's boat, and off they go. Once they get to the middle of the lake, Johnson pulls out a stick of dynamite, lights it, throws it out into the water, boom, dead fish everywhere. The game warden is stunned. He just sits and stares at Johnson in disbelief. And then the old fisherman pulls out another stick of dynamite, lights it, hands it to the warden, and says, "So you gonna just sit there or are you gonna fish?"

Ya know, there are times God has to prompt us to step out in faith. There have been many times his Holy Spirit has said to me, "So, Knappy-head, you gonna sit there or you gonna fish?" I'll bet you can say the same, huh? In other words, God brings a situation into our life that forces our hand and causes us to take an action we otherwise wouldn't. Or it could have been a circumstance that was uncomfortable or painful at the time, but coming out on the other side, we were wiser, stronger, more focused, more caring, and/or fully equipped for his next purpose in your life.

It would take a full day to share all the wonderful fallout from my six-year battle with cancer. But if I had to define the fallout, I would do it with one word: influence. There is no doubt that my influence is much more impacting and much more widespread because of the disease. I am more at peace and happier than any other moment in my life—in spite of cancer. In fact, because of cancer! How's that grab ya?

The book of James touches on the amount of influence one person can have when it says:

> Elijah was a man with a nature like ours, and he prayed earnestly that it would not rain; and it did not rain on the land for three years and six months. And he prayed again, and the heaven gave rain, and the earth produced its fruit.
>
> James 5:17–18, NIV

The prophet Elijah was a servant of God. Holiness was his character, but that was uncommon in his day. Ahab, the king, was a sinner of the blackest dye. His iniquity was glaring and infamous. Ahab made unto himself false gods. The people of Samaria were fallen like their monarch; Ahab's *influence* was felt throughout the land. The country had walked away from God. They had forsaken the God of Israel. They had forgotten that the scripture said, "The Lord thy God is one," (Deuteronomy 6:4, KJV) and they bowed in wicked idolatry before the idols of the heathens. In the time of Ahab, the scripture of Deuteronomy was coming true:

> "If you do not carefully observe all the words of this law that are written in this book, that you may fear this glorious and awesome name, the Lord your God then the Lord will bring upon you and your descendants extraordinary plagues—great and prolonged plagues—and serious and prolonged sicknesses."
>
> Deuteronomy 28:58–59, NIV

Darkness and sickness was covering the land. Moral decay, insensitivity to God and his standards, corrupt political power, open perversion and disobedience, had become the norm. Sound familiar, y'all?

But God did not forget his people. He sent one grain of salt, one ray of light, one warrior of God, one prophet, one watchman who stood in the watchtower to shout a warning, to save the people from utter destruction. Elijah had a divine influence upon history. The people knew him to be the prophet of the Lord. He had divine credentials. All of his prophecies had been fulfilled. They knew that he was a man sent from God and brought God's message to the people. Yet the scripture tells us: "Elijah was a man with a nature like ours." James 5:17, NIV

How much influence can one person have?

Another example of one man who stood in the watchtower—or in this case he was a voice calling in the wilderness—was John the Baptist. A man sent from God to proclaim the coming of God. He was clothed in camel's hair with a leather belt around his waist, surviving on a diet of locusts and wild honey (he would have fit in perfectly on *Duck Dynasty*). He shouted for all to hear: "Repent, for the kingdom of heaven is at hand!" (Matthew 3:2, KJV).

He was one grain of salt. He was one shard of light. He was sent to have an influence upon this world. Again, I ask: "How much influence can one man have?" The Bible tells us: "Then Jerusalem, all Judea, and all the region around the Jordan went out to him and were baptized by him in the Jordan, confessing their sins." (Matthew 3:5–6, NIV).

It is obvious that he had an influence, an impact, on the people he came in contact with.

A Peanuts cartoon showed Peppermint Patty talking to Charlie Brown. Peppermint Patty said to Charlie Brown, "Guess what, Chuck? Today was the first day of school, and I got sent to the principal's office. It was your fault, Chuck."

Charlie Brown responded, "My fault? How could it be my fault? Why do you say everything is my fault?"

Peppermint Patty answered, "You're my friend, aren't you, Chuck? Friends have an influence on one another. You should have been a better influence on me."

God says you and I can move a mountain by just having faith. If that is true—all of the Word is truth—then we have within us the ability to change the world for Jesus Christ! Begin with your circle of influence, one day at a time, fully surrendered, a bold ambassador. There are precious souls in the balance. You can do it. How do you begin? Simply look heavenward and say to the Lord, "Here am I send me!" Then get ready, God is about to light your dynamite!

Jesus Christ
by Coach Rock

Will you join me this morning in the greatest few minutes we can ever celebrate together? I just want us to think on Jesus. Isn't it mind blowing that this Jesus who is the Savior of Abraham, David, Noah, Moses, Paul, Peter, Billy Graham—this same Jesus is your Savior! Think about that for just a minute. He is the Savior of the apostle Paul and disciple Ted. His love, care, purpose, and desire to live in me is the same as he had for Paul. That's incredible! Don't mess with me, my Redeemer's got my back!

Jesus, Son of the living God (Matt 16:16), the Firstborn of Every Creature (Col 1:15), His Throne is forever and ever (Heb 1:8), Wonderful, Counselor, Mighty God, Everlasting Father, Prince of Peace (Isa 9:6), Emmanuel, God With Us (Matt 1:23), He is the Highest (Luke 1:76), Mighty in battle (Ps. 24:8), the Lord of Glory (1 Cor 2:8), the Resurrection and the Life! (John 11:25), And He Is Before All Things, And By Him All Things Consist (Col 1:17), The Almighty which is, and which was, and is to come! (Rev 1:8), the creator and upholder of all things (Col 1:16 & Heb 1:3), Alpha and Omega (Rev 1:8), The Life (1 John 1:2), The Word of Life (1 Jn 1:1), The Messenger of the Covenant

(Mal 3:1), The Son of Man (Mark 10:33), My Righteous Servant (Isa 53:11), Humbled Himself unto death (John 3), A Man of Sorrows (Isa. 53:3), And God has given Him a name above every name (Phil 2: 9 & 10), Jesus Christ, the same yesterday, today and forever (Heb 13:8), The Christ, the Savior of the World (John 4:42), The Lamb of God who is worthy of all Power, Riches, Strength, Honor, Glory and Blessing! (Rev 5:12), Shepherd of the sheep (Heb 13:20), The Way (John 14:6), True Vine (John 15:1), Tree of Life (Rev 2:7), The Bread of Life (John 6:35), The Rose of Sharon (S of S 2:1), Light of the world (John 8:12), Bright and Morning Star (Rev 22:16), The name of the Lord is a strong tower (Prov 18:10), A horn of Salvation (Luke 1:69), A refuge from the storm (Isa 25:4), The Real Rock! (1 Cor 10:4), A Living Stone (1 Pet 2:4), The Mercy Seat (Rom 3:25), Our Great High Priest (Heb 4:14), Our advocate to the Father (1 John 2:1), Gift of God (John 3:16), an Unspeakable gift (2 Cor. 9:15), The Faithful and True (Rev 19:11), He that is holy and He that is true (Rev 3:7), Holy, Holy, Holy (Isa 6:3), That in all things He might have the Preeminence (Col 1:18), The head over all things to the church (Eph 1:22), the author and finisher of our faith (Heb 2:2) King of Kings, Lord of Lords—He shall reign forever and evermore!

    Oh, the immeasurable hope and love Jesus lavishes on us. In that while we were yet sinners, Christ died for us! Draw near to Jesus, and he will draw near to you. He will never leave you or forsake you. *Jesus never fails.* Let all creation bow before him, lift holy hands, shout to the Lord. Call his name, his presence will fill you, bring you peace, calm your fear, light your path, part the seas, calm the storm, give you living water, clean your heart, heal your hurt, deliver right on time, give a supernatural increase, he will bring victory to our battle with the prince of the power of this world, he satisfies my soul, he brings my dry bones to life, he walks with me in the shadow of death, and he stands with me in the fiery furnace. And thanks be to God the Father—his (Jesus) mercy is new each and every morning.

> Give unto the Lord the glory due to His name; worship the Lord in the beauty of His holiness.
>
> Psalm 29:2, KJV

Jesus Followers Ain't Got to Go Far to Find Him
Rock Knapp

Okay, just finished up my Holy Hour (I read my Bible, pray, and then my Holy Hour is where I just sit quietly and invite the Holy Spirit to come and draw my thoughts on living that day surrendered to the will of God, etc.), and man, did the Holy Spirit lay some good stuff on me. He's the One pushing me to share it with you. So if you're reading this, then receive it as a direct tête-à-tête right from the Lord for you.

Are you born again? Have you received Jesus Christ into your heart as your Lord and Savior? Have you surrendered your life to him? Do you want more of him each day? Is he who you live for? Is it the desire of your heart that he must increase and you must decrease? Do you pray to be broken and empty in order for him to fill you with his spirit? Ya know y'all, I actually pray to be lonely so I chase his attention and his love with a real focus. And don't we all cry out for his mercy that is offered to us new each and every day. Ah, this risen Savior, he lives in me!

Did you just read that? He lives in me! I'm sitting there tonight just marveling at the truth and reality that Jesus is in me. It was quite a Holy Hour. I had such a joy whelp up inside me. I just had such an intense thanksgiving, praise, and worship celebration for my Lord. And right in the middle of that celebration, I stopped dead in my tracks. I went from exalting the Lord to examining my heart. I did a 180 and began looking at myself in light of Jesus living in me. It began with Colossians 1:10–12 where we read, "We pray this in order that you may live a life worthy of the Lord and please Him in every way." (NIV) Listen to what he has done for me.

> Living, He loved me
> Dying, He saved me
> Buried, He carried my sins far away
> Rising, He justified freely forever
> One day He's coming
> Oh glorious day, oh glorious day
>
> One day they led Him up Calvary's mountain
> One day they nailed Him to die on a tree
> Suffering anguish, despised and rejected
> Bearing our sins, my Redeemer is He
> Hands that healed nations, stretched out on a tree
> And took the nails for me

Do I walk worthy of that? Do I respond to him for all he has done for me by pleasing him in every way? Heavy stuff, isn't it? And on occasion, the Holy Spirit will by-pass the *still small voice*, and instead, his voice will fill my ears like thunder and the deafening sound of a cannon. This morning was one of those times.

Jesus Christ dwells in me! He lives inside of you! Jesus!

He was Crucified
He was Forsaken
He is Merciful
He is Faithful
He is Holy, Harmless
He is Undefiled
He is Separate
He is Perfect

He is Glorious
He is Mighty
He is Justified
He is Exalted
He is Risen
He is Glorified

My Maker
My Well-beloved
My Savior
My Hope
My Brother
My Portion
My Helper
My Physician
My Healer
My Refiner
My Purifier
My Lord, Master
My Servant
My Example
My Teacher
My Shepherd
My Keeper
My Feeder
My Leader
My Restorer
My Resting Place
My Passover
My Peace
My Wisdom
My Redemption
My All in All

The Lord of the universe lives inside me and you! And so you have to ask yourself right now: With such an incredible Resurrection living in me, is there enough evidence, change, impact to prove he is there inside me? Here is as true a statement as I will ever speak: I can't possibly have Jesus Christ inside me and not bear witness of it without radical change, continual manifestation, and our presence bringing a distinct sense of Christ everywhere we go. It's true! If we truly have this Jesus in us—in all his glory and power—it should completely swallow us. So if we were to take a poll with your family, friends, coworkers, and all those in your circle of influence, and take a survey, one that simply asks the question, "Do you see Jesus loud and clear in Rock Knapp?" Would you be nervous at the final tally? Made me do some self-examination this morning. Maybe you should do the same. Jesus is worth it. "Be strong in the Lord and in His mighty power" (Eph. 6:10, NIV). Let's be radical for Christ; turn him loose! Go, Jesus, go!

Say Yes to the Dress (and Much More)
by Coach Rock

I grew up in a denomination that loves the Bible. I believe they have the right doctrinal positions and are right on target with their hermeneutics. However, this same denomination, looking back now, had far too many don't and not enough do's. There are definite don'ts we need to hear and obey from Scripture, no doubt about it. But I can stay busy the next fifty years attempting to honor all the do's in the Bible. I'd rather focus on moving forward with commands to do than to have a mind-set of legalism where all I do is deny the abundant life and serving others (using Jesus as my model). In fact, let's break this puppy down, shall we?

Don't

- Sin (duh)
- Hate
- Envy
- Covet
- Lust
- Steal
- Cheat
- Gossip
- Put anything ahead of God (idols)
- Try and keep one foot in the world (lust of the flesh and pride of life)

Do's

- Love the Lord with all your heart and soul
- Pray without ceasing
- Meditate in the Word both day and night
- Tell others the Good News of the Gospel of Jesus Christ
- Get active serving others through the local church
- Give your first fruits to the Lord
- Trust him in every situation
- Surrender your will for his will
- Embrace the 7,000 promises in the Bible
- Pursue holiness

Notice you cannot find anything on these two abbreviated lists that addresses movies, dancing, alcohol, pants on women, long hair on men, mixed swimming, secular music, sacred music (contemporary like rap or heavy electric guitar versus hymns), how often to have communion, tattoos, righteous anger (when it applies), membership in secular organizations, secondary separation, on and on it goes. Now, I've got people telling me the Super Bowl and the Disney Channel are on the don't list. Some Christians believe in hell, some do not. The same can be said for evolution, same-sex marriages, abortion, is God masculine or feminine, praying to Mary or saints, on and on it goes. Seemingly, all 1,700 registered religions in the US lay claim to number 1 on the Bible Billboard! My sister, Tammy, once asked me in a very confused state of mind, "Ted, who's right and how do you know?"

Here is my answer for every single person out there: denominations are man-made. The Bible is God-made! If you will get in the Word, really meditate, memorize the Scripture, study it for yourself, pray constantly for God to direct your thoughts and order your steps, obey it, believe it, and pray for guidance and spiritual eyes of understanding, he will reveal truth to you. You'll be able to discern legalism from holiness. You'll find a lot of this nonsense to be inconsequential compared to pursuing his presence!

You want answers? Get in the Word of God, pray with the Holy Spirit. It will draw you near to God and God near to you. That will get us moving upward and forward, not spinning our wheels in the dung heap of don't.

Who Are You?
by Coach Rock

You aren't born as yourself. You're born facing a mass of possibilities, a mass of other people's ideas and preconceptions—and you have to mold a "self" by working through those raw materials.

—V. S. Naipaul

A human being is like a novel: until the last page you don't know how it will end. Or it wouldn't be worth reading.

—Yevgeny Zamyatin

Do not free a camel from the burden of his hump; you may free him from being a camel.

—G. K. Chesterton

If you hate a person, you hate something in him that is a part of you. What isn't part of ourselves doesn't disturb us.

—Herman Hess

My sense of my importance to myself is tremendous. I am all I have, to work with, to play with, to suffer and enjoy. It is not the eyes of others I am wary of, but my own.

—Noel Coward

I am a collection of water, calcium, and organic molecules called Carl Sagan.

—Carl Sagan

I don't know who my grandfather was. I am much more concerned to know what his grandson will be.

—Abraham Lincoln

Whenever two people meet, there are really six people present. There is each man as he sees himself, each as the other sees him, and each as he really is.

—William James

If I try to be like him, who will be like me?

—Yiddish Proverb

Know thyself? If I knew myself, I'd run away!

—Goethe

Life is a funny thing. There are just some mysteries that I'll never be able to bring to closure, much like making heads or tails out of all the above attempts at capturing the essence of human life.

Here's one of those mysteries: an apple will float in water, but a pear will sink. Why does one float and the other sink? How am I supposed to decide which is the more enjoyable aroma: chocolate or fresh ground coffee? Which do I choose as my favorite food: filet mignon or lobster? Why are you left-handed and I'm right-handed? I mean, who are we? What do I really know about myself? Well, there are a lot of mysteries out there that will never be revealed or resolved until the new heaven and new earth have arrived, and we can sit at the feet of the Creator and Controller of all that is and was and will be.

So I'm sitting there during my Holy Hour (something I do right after my devotions of reading the Bible and prayer time) in the very stillness of 2:00 a.m.—listening and chatting out loud to the Holy Spirit when I just sort of migrated to the "Who are you?" paradigm of self-analysis. Well, within one second, the Holy Spirit jumped in my lap (I know I sound nuts) and reminded me that my commitment this year, this new day, this very hour is to be thankful to the degree I stop to celebrate and for that celebration to lead me to great praise of the great God!

I sat there and began thinking through all that I should be thankful for and I moved seamlessly through the questions I had been reflecting over. Who am I? Who are you? Well, since we're both brothers and sisters, children of the same Father, let's do this together, then you can be thankful with me, celebrate with me (might include some dancing (just warning my Independent Baptist buddies), and we can praise him going into this new day.

> I am complete in Him who is the Head of all principality and power
>
> > Colossians 2:10
>
> I am alive with Christ.
>
> > Ephesians 2:5

I am free from the law of sin and death.

Romans 8:2

I am far from oppression, and fear does not come near me.

Isaiah 54:14

I am born of God, and the evil one does not touch me.

1 John 5:18

I am holy and without blame before Him in love.

Ephesians 1:4; 1 Peter 1:16

I have the mind of Christ.

1 Corinthians 2:16; Philippians 2:5

I have the peace of God that passes all understanding.

Philippians 4:7

I have the Greater One living in me; greater is He Who is in me than he who is in the world.

1 John 4:4

You Know What?
by Coach Rock

You know what? I don't want to title this morning's devotional. I just want to share some things bouncing around in my spirit the last few days. I've been trying to define it, package it, but it won't conform to the typical *Lifeway* outline or an *Our Daily Bread* tidy package. It's just a mixed bag of principles and truths seasoned with some common sense and years of experience. Vituperative exclamations rarely achieve desired results, but at the same time, if you'll let me, I'd like to at least poke you with a stick, pull no punches, hit you hard right between the eyes. Why? Because there lies within each of us so much more, enough to change all the world around us. I don't want you to get a blessing from this, so what! I want you to *make things happen* for the glory of your God! So let me begin.

Andrew Carnegie once said, "As I grow older, I pay less attention to what men say. I just watch what they do." So true. Like I said, poke you with a stick. Here she comes:

- When is the last time you discovered resources in places others thought barren?
- You found prospects where others failed to find them?
- You created opportunity where others thought none existed?
- Come on now, last time you took the average and made it exceptional?
- When's the last time you went a whole day without making an excuse?

Remember now, this whole ramble is about stimulating me and you to *make things happen* for the glory of the King. Well, in order to do that, it would seem to me you would constantly be looking to *see and seize opportunity*. I've learned that anybody can recognize opportunity after it has passed them by! Here's a reminder: Opportunity is seldom labeled. Don't sit back and wait! I'm not. I've got limited time, and I'm pressing hard to fill all my time with, "Here am I, send me!" I have three friends who fascinate me. One is Drew Neidhammer. Andrew played quarterback for me in the mid-80s and through the years has become one of my dearest and most trusted friends. This dude *never* stops—perpetual motion 24×7. He is constantly dreaming big, and then without an invitation or sleeping on it, he jumps off the high dive right into the action plan. As a result and here is really where I'm headed today, he has such great impact on others and gets things done that others fail to do. The same is true for Marla Chambless. Marla is the mother of one of my boys down at Sherwood Christian Academy in Albany, Georgia. She is the wife of a "get after it" farmer, the mother of four children (all at home), my most dependable booster club member, full-time attorney, and always doing something above and beyond to help others. Drew is a highly successful sales executive, author, speaker, coach, and radio show host. Marla has such a heart for other people, and with all she has accomplished, her main focus is serving others and that my friend is drawing people to Jesus. I think of Mark Tidwell, another former quarterback (my first one to be exact and the trigger man to lead us to a state championship too!). He just had a very serious surgery, and only three to four weeks after being sliced open from stem to stern, he was out sharing the Good News of the Gospel of Jesus Christ to the Kell football team yesterday (Mark is with FCA) and saw twenty-five boys give their hearts to Christ! Mark is battling for his life with colon cancer and still making things happen, leaving a mark. What's your excuse again?

You know why most never do anything great in life? Opportunity knocks on the front door, but they are in the backyard looking for four-leaf clovers! Answer the door!

Another thought bouncing around in my head—hang on, I'm grabbing my poking stick. Here she comes again right in the ribs: *How much of your ability and potential to influence others for eternity are you using?* Yea, I'm talking to you. Don't make me get up. You realize there are two basic reasons people don't know Jesus as their Lord. Yep, two. They have never met a Christian (that's one), and here comes the stick, secondly, they have met a Christian! Influence is no small matter, y'all. Leadership, it's in you! God put it there. You have all the tools; you are equipped and empowered with ability and potential of a supernatural nature. Lead! Walk on water, feed 5,000, move a mountain, *or how about mentor and serve others?* Two things I know about watching leaders: they always have somewhere they're going, and they are able to influence others to go with them. Get a map, get a plan, and get off your butt (one of those vituperative exclamations I say to myself every day too!).

Winding down: who do you hang with? Let's evaluate your friends, your sphere of influence, yes, even as adults. So often the people around us determine to some degree our success. The character, attitudes, integrity, example of those around us *does* spark our character and can motivate us to *full capacity of making things happen*. We all need friends (brothers and sisters in Christ) who, when we are together, create iron sharpening iron. Find folks who will take you to a higher level of achievement, effectiveness, and ministry. Then you go do likewise, the principle of duplication.

Man, we need *doers* of the Word more than ever. Last thought: I watch those churches that have not grown at all the last twenty years or so, just frozen in time. My theory why? Every stinkin' one is a staff-led church. No one is developing leaders, *doers*. And so they just sit, soak, sour. You, you, you, not the others reading this you have a greatness in you designed by God himself. So *go make things happen today, would ya?* Go make a miracle; go tar and feather the impossible; tell one about Jesus.

Give Yourself a Hand!
by Coach Rock

> I praise you because I am fearfully and wonderfully made; your works are wonderful...My frame was not hidden from you when I was made in the secret place. When I was woven together in the depths of the earth, your eyes saw my unformed body. All the days ordained for me were written in your book before one of them came to be.
>
> Psalm 139:14–16, NIV

The human body is the most unique and complex organism in the universe. Let's look at the brain. The human brain is an amazing organ, fearfully and wonderfully made. It has the ability to learn, reason, and control so many automatic functions of the body such as heart rate, blood pressure, and breathing, and to maintain balance to walk, run, stand, and sit, all while concentrating on something else. Computers can outdo the human brain in raw calculating power, but are primitive when it comes to performing most reasoning tasks. The brain also has an amazing ability to adapt.

Consider the single fertilized cell of a newly conceived human life. From that one cell within the womb develop all the different kinds of tissues, organs, and systems, all working together at just the right time in an amazingly coordinated process. An example is the hole in the septum between the two ventricles in the heart of the newborn infant. This hole closes up at exactly the right time during the birth process to allow for the oxygenation of the blood from the lungs, which does not occur while the baby is in the womb and is receiving oxygen through the umbilical cord. I'll never forget being in the delivery room when Teddy (our oldest) was born. Just as he was getting slapped on the booty, I hit the floor like a ton of bricks! But it wasn't the blood, etc., that sent me to the canvas like getting hit by Mike Tyson; honestly, it was the wonder of it all—I was overwhelmed at God's handiwork.

Further, the body's immune system is able to fight off so many enemies and restore itself from the smallest repair (even repairing bad portions of DNA) to the largest (mending bones and recovering from major accidents). Yes, there are diseases that will eventually overcome the body as we age (I'm the poster boy), but we have no idea how many times through a lifetime that our immune systems have saved us from certain death.

The functions of the human body are also incredible. The ability to handle large heavy objects and to also carefully manipulate a delicate object without breaking it is also amazing. We can shoot a bow with the arrow repeatedly hitting a distant target, peck away quickly at a computer keyboard without thinking about the keys, crawl, walk, run, twirl around, climb, swim, do somersaults and flips, and perform simple tasks such as unscrewing a lightbulb, brushing our teeth, and lacing up our shoes—again without thinking. The function of the digestive tract and the related organs, the longevity of the heart, the formation and function of nerves and of blood vessels, the cleansing of the blood through the kidneys (again, poster boy), the complexity of the inner and middle ear, the sense of taste and smell, and so many other things we barely understand—each one is a marvel and beyond man's ability to duplicate. I just read in my almanac this past week that the human liver performs over 500 different functions! Truly, we are fearfully and wonderfully made. How grateful we are to know the Creator—through his Son, Jesus Christ—and to marvel not only at his knowledge, but also at his love!

But wait, I got more! Hold your hand up in front of your face. Look at it, look at it very closely—why—because it is the only one divinely designed by God in all the history of mankind. No other human being has ever had the same exact hand as yours! God thought through every microscopic cell as he was writing down "you" in his book (v16). There is no one like you…ever. One of a kind. You are irreplaceable, unique, intended, calculated, and highly anticipated by your Creator (who made sure you would reflect his image!).

So? Have you figured it out yet? Has it even crossed your mind why God made just one of you in all of history? Well, it is quite simple yet powerfully profound. You were divinely designed because God has a purpose for you, and you are the only person in all creation and all time who can complete the purpose God created you for. You have a rare purpose, a one-of-a-kind purpose, a deliberate divine destiny. Jeremiah 29:11 makes it very clear that God has a future for you—one that will give you hope and one that will prosper your faithfulness to his purpose. I said all these things this morning to focus on one simple thought:

In order to know the plan, know the planner! Draw near to God, and he will draw near to you. Get in the Word, pray. Your purpose awaits you.

Excellence over Acceptability
by Coach Rock

II Tim. 2:15 tells us to study the Word until we're excellent at knowing it and sharing it. Cigar-puffing Spurgeon said it simply, "Be excellent in the Word." Amen, bro.

The Scripture screams aloud the recurring theme that whatsoever your hands find to do, do it with all your might. Be a world record holder. Competitive excellence requires 100 percent all of the time. Swindoll says, "Go ahead and try maintaining excellence by setting your standards at 92%. or even 95%. People today feel their doing fine so long as they get somewhere near it. Excellence gets reduced to acceptable, and before long, acceptable doesn't seem worth the sweat if you can get by with adequate. After that, mediocrity is only a breath away!" Amen, bro.

After thirty years of coaching football, after the weekend of incredible finishes in the NCAAs, it is very obvious to me there is no such thing as luck. Willa Foster said this, "Quality is never an accident; it is always the result of high intention, sincere effort, intelligent direction and skillful execution, it represents the wise choice of many alternatives." I've always said it this way: "Your practice doesn't make perfect. Practice makes permanent. Perfect practice makes perfect. We prepare to perfection, we'll play to perfection."

But let me give you a heads up this day. *Watch out for the little foxes!* In the Song of Solomon, chapter 2 and verse 15, we're clearly commanded to "Take us the foxes, the little foxes that spoil the whole vine." What does that mean? A runner from the USA competed in our last Olympic marathon (26.1 distance race), and he failed miserably to place near the top. He said in an interview that he almost quit the race. When asked why, he said, "Because of the sand in my shoes!" Profound. Listen, my brother and my sister, don't neglect the details! It takes a lot of little things to add up to 100 percent.

One last thing about excellence, even for adults. I have taught my children and thousands of other children this Bible principle/ life axiom: We become like those we spend time with. So quit running with that bucket of blue crabs and find those Christ followers who will be as iron sharpening iron, helping us to greater capacity and to a higher level of achievement, effectiveness, and ministry (throwing the right seed in the right ground and at the right time). Okay, back to the bucket of blue crabs, if you drop just one in the bucket, he will immediately and effortlessly just climb right out. But put two…four…ten…one hundred in the bucket and not one will crawl out! They will drag one another down so that none of them can get away. Unsuccessful people act the same way; you are not one of them!

So excellence is a choice. Choose it right now (Eph. 6:10; Habakkuk 3:19; 2 Thess. 3:3; Phil. 3:13–14). I am blessed to have one man from our church who has taken on the responsibility of becoming a 100 percent friend as I walk through the valley, the Lord spoke to Dave and it was a perfect fit from the beginning. Dave has encouraged me, been a consistent man of the Word, and is a wonderful example of a doer of the Word, not just a hearer. I could never put into words how much Dave and Debbie mean to me. I am hoping to do the same for someone too. Get the sand out of your shoes and come on, let's go on a run, maybe we'll see ole' Gump along the way?

Fire, Fire, Fire
by Coach Rock

When I went to Bible college, I suppose it would be an understatement to say I was a little rough around the edges; here's one of hundreds of examples. My second period class my first semester of my freshman year, I had Speech. I had a professor I really enjoyed, and she was one of the few faculty members who encouraged me to live for the Lord; most were too busy keeping a critical eye on my shenanigans (as they should have). Well, as I remember, our professor taught us in the first week of Speech that when standing before people, we should always begin with an "attention getter." Just what I needed to hear. I'm gonna say about a week into classes, we had to pass around a hat and every student had to pick a folded piece of paper from the hat. Written on the paper was one word. We then had to go the front and give a two-minute speech on that one word. When you finished, the class had to guess your word. I had the word *fire*, and I knew immediately what I would do. Remember the attention getter? Well, I did. I got up walked to the classroom door and there next to the door on the wall was the fire alarm. I opened our door, I yelled *fire* to the top of my lungs (we were on the third floor of the academic classroom wing), and pulled the alarm. People scrambled everywhere—total chaos. I received 145 demerits (expelled at 150 per semester), was "campused" (grounded from leaving campus till the next semester), and I got to have a little visit later in the day with Dr. Cedarholm (college founder and president).

That is the way it will be at the end of the world. The angels will come and separate the wicked people from the godly, throwing the wicked into the fire. There will be weeping and gnashing of teeth. And I find myself once again yelling to the top of my lungs to all who read this: fire, fire, fire!

I speak today to the seeker, those looking for answers and purpose for their lives. They believe in God, but are unable to put the pieces of the puzzle together when it comes to the plan of salvation. They are genuinely seeking more than themselves, am I right? It is so simple to secure God's salvation. Simply trust Jesus as your Savior, his finished work on the cross where he died for your sins and mine. Receive him into your heart today (John 3:16; Rev. 3:20; John 1:12), repent and ask forgiveness of all sin and make him Lord of your life. Oh, man, will heaven throw a party (without the fear of demerits!)!

If you reject him, you gamble with being condemned to hell. Yea, I know, it ain't cool to talk about hell anymore. Prosperity and comfort are much more popular subjects. I don't care. I do not want you in a burning cell of solitary confinement forevermore. Hell is a place of eternal darkness. You see, God is light. At the moment you are cast from his presence, there is no light. Darkness becomes your eternal companion. The Bible says it is a bottomless pit; in hell, there will be a sense of falling, pushed from the cliffs of glory into perpetual darkness, forever falling, falling, falling farther from God. The most horrible aspect of hell is no more chances! It's over. There is coming a time when you will reject Jesus for the last time.

When Professor T. H. Huxley, the father of agnosticism, came to the end of his life, the nurse attending him said that as he lay dying, the great skeptic suddenly looked up at some sight invisible to mortal, and staring a while, whispered at the last, "So it is true!" And he died. Stalin had a daughter; she gave the account of his lying on his death bed when he suddenly opened his eyes and looked at the people in the room. It was a look of unutterable horror and anguish. Then he lifted his left hand and pointed at something and dropped it and died and was ushered into hell.

Is your name in the Book of Life? Is Jesus your Savior and Lord? (John 3:16, John 1:12, Rev.3:20). Oh, how he loves you.

Good Old Cancer
by Coach Rock

Good old cancer, what a guy. He sneaks up on me, decides not to give me any warning that life was about to change in as dramatic fashion as Hannah Montana morphed overnight into Miley

Cyrus. I mean one day, life is as good as it can get, and the next day, life becomes a horror story that isolates you from even your family. Stunned, confused, and wondering what I did to provoke God to such punishment. This wasn't the breakup of a marriage, this wasn't losing custody of my children. It was a death sentence. God was going to let me die. My response? Brokenness.

In his book, *Beautiful Outlaw*, John Eldredge makes quite a profound observation in direct assessment of our one on one relationship with Jesus. Think about this: So much emphasis is put on us in regards to what we think about him. The real question here is what does Jesus think about me? Watch now, most of us (Christians) suffer from some measure of brokenness. And here is the kicker, we interpret Jesus through our brokenness. Let's use my cancer as our example or illustration of this all too common misunderstanding that Satan uses to torment us on a daily basis. With my death sentence comes brokenness. My brokenness can be best defined by feeling like I am not good enough for Jesus, I find it hard to believe he loves me, I feel like I'm always disappointing him, I have little to offer so he seems so distant, yes, he is loving—we all know that, but with me, he seems disengaged. I'm not doing enough. I'm not loving him enough. My past has severed my chances of ever having an intimate and abiding relationship with Christ. So the Jesus I have in my head really isn't the Jesus in my heart! I have allowed my brokenness to make me paranoid about what Jesus thinks about me.

Now, if any of this is kicking you dead in the gut, listen carefully!

Tell Jesus what you think he thinks of you. Ask him if it's true. Ask him to free you of such mental imprisonment. Ask him to heal your past wounds. Come running to your Lord. He waits with open arms. He will restore your spirit, clean your heart, and renew your strength like that of an eagle. You will take flight, you will inhale his grace with each new breath. And your brokenness will be transformed into freedom to live the abundant life all the while focused on becoming an absolute slave to the will of God and living to bring glory on earth to your Master, Redeemer, and best friend Jesus.

How do I know these things? Ah, remember our old friend Peter?

Talk about broken! While Jesus was being tried and tortured, Peter denies him three times! Can you imagine the horror that went through Peter when he renounces Christ and the rooster crowed, and Jesus with his face beaten almost to the point he was unrecognizable, and yet he looks up and he looks Peter dead in the eyes. My God, it had to be the lowest moment of Peter's whole life! We do know he ran outside and wept; brokenness becomes his great tormentor. And then, oh, I am thrilled to share the real Jesus right now! Jesus, there on the shoreline of the Sea of Tiberius, fills the nets for Peter and company. The second Peter sees the impossible catch in the nets and John shouts to the heavens, "Jesus!" Old Pete immediately jumps from the boat and swims straight into the arm of his waiting Lord. For in the end, it is easy to see, y'all—healing our brokenness is exactly what Jesus came to do!

Faith = Spiritual Eyes of Understanding = Relationship!
by Coach Rock

Okay, I'm about to bite off more than I can chew I think, but what I'm about to share with you *is* my reality, my journey, my joy, and a best friend who is the same yesterday, today, and forever. No one will ever be able to separate me from his love. He walks with me and talks with me, and his still small voice has no rival. In fact, I talk more to my risen Savior than any other person on earth. He speaks to me through his Word, through the Holy Spirit, and through his abiding presence. All that screams just one thing: *relationship!*

Last night, I attended a Super Bowl party, and toward the end of the night, I found myself listening to a semi-debate between three men that were all very superior to me intellectually (Yea, I know, the GEICO pig can make that claim). I mean, it was an impressive discussion; the topic was creation versus evolution. I didn't open my mouth (yes, I had six classroom hours of creationism in Bible college, but I'm telling you these guys were way out there), I stayed in the bullpen.

As their discussion began to finally wind down, one of the gentlemen kept coming back to the premise that neither biblical creation or evolution could be proved and that it all comes down to faith, and faith isn't something that can prove anything. It's just faith, deciding to believe. Well, I listened to this line of logic, and just as I was about to burst, my wife tugged on my arm and said it was time to go, school tomorrow. I turned to walk away when all of a sudden the Lord stopped me and simply whispered, "Speak." I turned back around and said, "Can I tell you men why faith isn't a driving force in my life, the life of a dying man?" For the next twenty minutes, I held serve while they never spoke or moved a muscle. The Spirit of God fell on all of us.

I began by saying how essential faith is to the Christian, and it was by faith I trusted in the finished work of Jesus for my salvation. But men, the Bible gives us enough to anchor our faith with strong evidence, regardless of the subject. Let's take a look at some examples: George Washington did not die from a throat disease (as the history books tell us), he died from bleeding to death. He had strep, which brought on a fever of course. The medical profession of his day had the practice of bleeding a fever; the blood was the culprit. So they bled him two or three times a day until he died. May I ask you what one medical procedure of modern-day medicine has saved more lives than any other procedure? Blood transfusions. In the book of Lev.17:11, Moses writes that "the life of the flesh is in the blood." (KJV) And did you know in the book of Job (arguably the oldest book in the

Bible), the prophet wrote these words: "The earth is a sphere suspended upon nothing." Now, what is the official scientific shape of the earth? Yep, a sphere. And the earth is tilted on its axis just perfectly to support our life and keep the sun from burning us all up. How was it tilted? God spoke it, so it was! Galileo invented the telescope; he declared there were too many stars to even try counting them. In fact, he said it would be impossible to count them all. The Bible says the stars in the sky are like the sand on the seashore, "without number." About twenty years ago, we sent the Hubble into space, and it was able to see other galaxies. Scientists said there were too many to count, without number! Y'all beginning to see a pattern here? Long before man figured it out, God wrote it! I could go on and on with example after example. Once we've exercised our faith, it begins to grow—bigger and stronger. Our spiritual eyes of understanding are opened to see the hand of God as well as hear his still small voice. We experience his answering prayer, working miracles, changing lives, etc. After a while, our faith almost takes a backseat to our actual relationship with Christ.

I no longer walk by faith. I walk by my Savior in a daily and constant relationship. His abiding and his presence are real. I've gone from faith to evidence to relationship, and *knowing* he is real, his Word is absolute truth, and the Holy Spirit directs my life.

So yes, faith is still very important and necessary to live as God desires, but, folks, there is nothing more real, more true, more sure than my relationship with Jesus. Why he loves a wretch like me—oh, happy day!

Ten Devotionals
by Drew Neidhammer

Drew Neidhammer has written a book titled *Proverbs for Football*. Drew played quarterback on 1986 Riverdale Baptist team located in Upper Marlboro, Maryland. He was a stellar wide out through high school until his senior year. He made the sacrifice for the team. He presently is a sales executive with FedEx, but for twelve years, he was a high school football coach. In fact, Drew holds the distinguished honor of being the first head football coach of home school football in the nation. He started the phenomenon that now has teams in almost all fifty states.

1. The wise hears and increases learning; and understanding one gets wisdom.

Proverbs 1:5

I try to read as much as I can. Some books for fun, some are historical and many are often religious in nature. It fascinates me what others read, and if you are around me long enough, be sure I will ask you, "Have you read anything good lately?" What surprises me more often than not are the mostly men who respond, "I don't read," and then snicker like it is some badge of honor. You don't read? What? I wish there were two of me so one of me could always be reading!

Would you snicker at Peyton Manning if he asked you if you read? Here is one of the greatest of all times that reads and studies insistently to get better at his craft. You see it doesn't matter if you are preparing for a football game, learning a new medical procedure, or getting ready to stand in the pulpit, read, learn, and understand as much as you can. The more you learn, the more God will show you in the world around you. Aren't you just the slightest bit curious about his awesome creation?

2. Go to the ant, sluggard; consider his ways and be wise.

Proverbs 6:6, KJV

Ants work. They don't whine, complain, or improvise doing their own thing. They never stop, and they accomplish more as a group than anyone could ever imagine. That almost sounds like a team! They will accomplish their tasks by endless repetition as mundane as it may seem and a coach, boss, or even a parent might do the same thing. Drill after drill, day after day, over and over again. It isn't until the first game that the hard work of summer two-a-days all pays off. The offensive line fires off the ball as a single solid wall of pain. Running backs hit the hole at full speed, never looking for the ball that has been placed in their gut. And the quarterback has his steps so perfectly timed that he can do it blindfolded. It isn't always athletic ability that gets you to the championship, but more of endless repetition and precise execution. Whenever you see someone being crowned a champion, know that it wasn't just handed to them. It was preceded by days, months, and years of hard work. Trust me when I say that God is preparing you for something big. Don't look for the prize at the end; just look at the task at hand.

3. Give instruction to a wise man, and he will be yet wiser: teach a just man, and he will increase in learning.

Proverbs 9:9, KJV

What does it mean to have a teachable spirit? Are you coachable? Can people give you instruction or even criticism without you getting upset or offended? Are you walking around with an enormous chip on your shoulder, just waiting for somebody to get into your space? If you surround yourself with people that truly care about you, you won't mind when they try to help you. If they love you, they want you to better yourself. There is so much you can learn from people by just asking questions. I remember my mother once told me that she, "didn't care if I wanted to be a garbage man. Just find the most successful garbage man you can and ask him a million questions. Do what they did to become successful." Here is a test you might not want to take: when you have to put something together, do you look at the directions or try to wing it on your own? Maybe you better not answer that. God makes us a wonderful promise. If we ask for wisdom, he grants it to us every time. But you just might be surprised how he gives it to you.

4. He who works with a lazy hand becomes poor, but the hand of the hard worker makes him rich.

Proverbs 10:4, NIV

How hard do you work? Do you put in 100 percent into what you are doing or do you slide by with the absolute minimum amount of effort to just barely get it done? I am asking this about school, work, and at home. What is it that drives you? Is it being the best or just skating through life good enough for you? I know that you have been told that, "You can't get something for nothing," but it sure seems like it for some. There are people that appear to have it easy. They have rich parents who hand them everything. Or maybe, they are the boss's son. What will end up happening is that eventually it will catch up with them. I often tell people that you most likely will never be cut from a team or be fired from work if you just show up, on time, every day. Just showing up on time is more than what 90 percent of the workforce does each year. I heard that former President George Bush use to say, "If you show up on time, you are 15 minutes late!" Get up, get up early. Get to where you have to go early. You just might catch the person making all of the decisions with nobody to talk to but you!

5. The integrity of the upright shall guide them; but the crookedness of traitors shall destroy them.

Proverbs 11:3, KJV

Every now and then, on some teams (sports and work), the issue of integrity comes up. Satan will try and destroy any group that is making a positive impact on those around them. Unfortunately, it is happening in marriage and in our homes. There might even be so-called friends of yours trying to undermine those making a difference. Taking something that is good and tearing it down almost seems like an American sport! We quickly build up an underdog and then tear them down as soon as they reach the top. We love to see the rich and famous doing the perp walk in handcuffs. Somehow, it makes us feel better when we see the beautiful fall from grace. Pray that God guards your heart and that never happens. Pray that he puts a hedge of protection around all that you do because as Christians, we are always at war when we are doing the will of God. Ask God to give you wisdom and discernment to root out those trying to destroy what God has ordained.

6. A soft answer turns back wrath, but a hurtful word stirs up anger.

Proverbs 15:1, KJV

There is a lot of yelling in sports. I used to tell my players that I will be yelling on game night for two reasons: First, because you have to hear me over the crowd. Secondly, I have a theory that game day adrenalin makes you go deaf! What I needed to learn is that I couldn't treat my parents, children, or wife the way I treat my football players. My wife would often remind me, "I'm not your assistant and the kids are not lazy linemen!" Boy, did she know her football. One harsh word to her or the children at the wrong time can affect their lives forever. You could say something in anger that a person will remember the rest of their lives. Pray that God will take control of your tongue.

7. The refining pot is for silver, and the furnace for gold; but the Lord trieth the hearts.

Proverbs 17:3, KJV

Are you going through a difficult time right now? Are you being pushed further than you think you can go? A coach's job is to push you past the point where you can take yourself. Football is hard, hot, and exhausting, but it can be very rewarding, just like being a Christian. What coaches are doing on the outside, God is doing on the inside. He comes into our lives and gives us a new heart. Then we spend a lifetime trying to match our outward actions to our changed heart. It is not what you can do for God, but what he has done and is trying to do for you on the inside. Hopefully, your actions will match your heart. The only way a diamond can be created is through time, heat, and pressure.

8. Do not envy evil men, nor desire to be with them. For their heart studies violence, and their lips talk of mischief.

Proverbs 24:1–2, KJV

People love old gangster movies and especially the newer mafia movies/TV shows like *Scarface* and *The Sopranos*. There has to be something exciting about bad guys or Solomon wouldn't have written about them over 3,000 years ago. I think it is all about an element of danger and living on the edge that draws us to them. Most moms and women in our lives may never understand why guys love an element of danger. But there is a difference in seeking a thrill legally and breaking the law. Being tough isn't running around with a gun. To me, it is more like standing for four seconds in the pocket, returning a punt, or running a drag across the middle. Do you really want a thrill? Do you want to be the toughest dude at your school or at work? Stand up and claim to be a man of God and profess that you have made Jesus Christ your personal Savior. You will definitely be challenged. And that is a rush and feeling that most of the men in this world will never get the chance to experience.

9. All the words of my mouth are in righteousness; nothing twisted or perverse in them.

   Proverbs 8:8, KJV

Tommy was a hero of mine. You have never heard of him because he only played high school football. He was a senior captain when I was a sophomore—a slashing tailback with some of the quickest feet I have ever seen. But it wasn't his football prowess that I looked up to. It was the way he encouraged me and went out of his way to help me as I was learning the game. He made me want to be a better player, the true definition of a teammate. It wasn't just me he encouraged; it was all of the underclassmen. What would it mean to you if somebody came alongside and encouraged you? He always had a positive word, always something good to say. There are times when life is good and you don't have a care in the world. Then there are other times when you are discouraged and you feel like your entire life is crashing in. That is why it is so important to have a personal relationship with Jesus Christ. He came to earth as a man, not only to die for our sins, but also to be an encouragement to us so that we know he understands the struggles and temptations we go through on a daily basis.

10. Where no counsel is, the people fall; but in the multitude of counselors there is safety.

    Proverbs 11:14, KJV

It is called a Circle of Counsel. Simply, it is a group of people that you can count on for advice and should be made up of several different types of people. I recommend at least one pastor/counselor, a teacher, coach, parent(s), and a parent of a friend. A team captain or peer that is a couple of years older than you should also be considered. What you are doing is simply gathering information and opinions from people that can see things from different angles and perspectives. That does *not* mean you are going to do exactly what that say. It just means you compile this information so you can make an educated decision. I once had a coach that allowed the captains to decide whether a player would be kicked off the team or not. He broke a team rule, and the coach said it was our team. As one of the captains, I was glad to get the perspective of my peers and others. I also spent time in prayer. You see, the Great Counselor and the Prince of Peace wants you to seek him out, call upon his name for everything, regardless of how small. Many times, he will use the godly advice of others to answer your questions.

David: Murderer and Adulterer / A Man after God's Own Heart? Connect Those Dots!
by Coach Rock

I have certain Bible stories and Bible characters that I find mesmerizing. David is one of them. I've been in several fights as a young adult. Of course, these days, my ninth grade daughter has to carry the laundry basket for me and help me up and down stairs. Anyway, there was a time I was a lot like Travolta in the movie *Michael* (the archangel) and his doing "battle" with the bull out in the pasture, remember that scene? Once I was in a restaurant, seated in a no smoking area (many years ago), there was a man smoking in the booth next to us. I asked him politely to please put the cigarette out or go outside and smoke. He ignored me, not for long. I got up, walked to his booth, took his cigarette, dropped it in his coffee, punched him in the head, knocked him cold, got arrested. I must admit, I was quite dimwitted in times past. I failed to bear the mark of a Christian or respond to opportunities to honor the Lord with godly behavior. I seemed to return wrong with wrong (sin with sin). In the first few years of our marriage, I put Shari in harm's way by fist fighting at the drop of a hat. I suppose the word *idiot* and *stupid* would best apply in those early '80s. I can't imagine acting so foolishly today. I hardly remember that Ted. It is hard to even share it with you…embarrassingly so.

Why share that nonsense? Well, one of those Bible characters I find most interesting is David. His life has been a good blueprint for me to follow. I think the Forrest Gump line applies quite well to both myself and David in our younger days, "Stupid is as stupid does." Here was a guy who committed adultery and murder, talk about rogue behavior! As I get older, I hear more and more tales of skeletons in the closet from almost every Christian I know. Seems we all have past behavior that has fallen short of the mark of Christ-like behavior, embarrassingly so.

So where am I going with this mess? Well, I'd like to uncover what appears to be a real oxymoron of the Old Testament: God called David, a man after God's own heart. Come again? Let me remind you, God, he was a murderer and an adulterer! How can this possibly be and how does it apply to my life, and to you reading this, how does it apply to you? Let's look at David from God's vantage point.

In Acts 13:22, God says of David, "I have found David, son of Jesse a man after my own heart; he will do everything I want him to do." (NIV) If you read 1 and 2 Chronicles and 1 and 2 Kings, you'll see that David's life was a portrait of success and failure. Hmmm, sounds familiar? David was far from perfect and yet God identifies him as a cut above others because his heart was pointed to God.

In part 2, I will give you the key elements to being a man/woman after God's own heart. In spite of our early days of sin, self, and Satan, God is able to replace our filthy rags with robes of righteousness and a clean heart! This is exciting stuff!

Dissecting David and Discerning the Dots
Part 2

Salt is an interesting dinner guest. It is a combination of sodium and potassium. But when you separate the two, the potassium becomes a stand-alone poison. David was a man after God's own heart, but had an episode of runaway lust and chased down the curvaceous Bathsheba. He slept with her, committing adultery, and trumped that hideous act by plotting the death of her husband, Uriah. In my opinion, David was a slime ball and deserved to be executed by way of public hanging.

Good news, my people, my opinion does not count for squat in God's economy. Thank goodness, I'm not in charge or I'd have already muddied the water with something contrary to divine law by introducing spiritual insurance with Knappcare. In other words, only God can do what God can do! His thoughts are so much higher than our thoughts. His ways are so much better than our ways. He is perfectly just. So when God says that David was a man after God's own heart, he was 100 percent right. So let's connect the dots.

1. David had an incredible faith and trust in God. It was evident as a young teen that David had a supernatural trust in the Father, and he should! The youngin' had hand-to-hand combat with a bear and with a lion and killed them both. This was superman of the shepherds! So when it came time to volunteer to fight the most feared warrior on the planet, David did not flinch or blink. In fact, he started running at Goliath. He knew God would give him the victory. It was such an elevated trust—it produced elevated results and pronounced to the world an elevated God! 1 Sam. 17:37 said, "The Lord who delivered me from the paw of the lion and from the paw of the bear will deliver me from the hand of the Philistine."

(kjv) So if you want to be a man after God's own heart, then I suggest you put all your faith and trust in the God of David.
2. David absolutely loved the Word of God. He had this incredible appetite for meditating on the precepts and commands of God. Of the 150 Psalms, David wrote over half of them. We see just how much he loved God's Word in Ps. 119: 47–48, niv, "For I delight in your commands because I love them. I lift up my hands to your commands, which I love, and I meditate on your decrees." The kicker here is David's total adoration for meditating on his devotional throughout the day. That is exactly what God wants from us today! Read Ps. 119:2–3, niv, "Blessed are they who keep His statutes and seek Him with all their hearts. They do nothing wrong; they walk in His ways." Make it a habit to apply the Word to every situation of life.
3. David was truly thankful. What jumps out at me about this characteristic of David is his consistency. Chip will know this (if he did his homework): David's life was marked by great seasons of peace and prosperity as well as fear and despair. But through it all, he never stopped giving thanks to God. It was David who wrote our text from Thanksgiving, Psalms 100, "Enter His gates with thanksgiving and His courts with praise." A grateful heart is a heart after God's heart.
4. David was truly repentant. The mighty fall hard and David was no exception. His adultery multiplied into lying and murder. 2 Sam. 12:13, Ps. 51:1–2: these verses capture David's very sincere prayer of repentance. Someone with a heart for God cannot hide their sin or can they justify it. They confess it and turn from it.

Well, there ya go. You can wrap this whole thing in bacon by simply understanding that it is by grace, we are saved to the uttermost. It is not a result of our own righteousness. None of us come close to having our picture hung in the heavenly Hall of Fame. And I hope each of us walks away from this devotional being reminded of two things: first, stand guard over your heart. Never think you've arrived spiritually. Glance several times a day at those feet of clay. Secondly, God loves right through our disloyalty, debauchery, and doubts. What a miraculous, unconditional, immeasurable love God has for us.

What Do You See in the Mirror?
by Coach Rock

Insecure as you think of Judgment Day? Lacking confidence? Living your life without a sense of destiny? Looking for that Christ-confidence that allows you to be used in a great way for the kingdom? May I put it in coaching vernacular: stop sitting on the bench and go get in the game! Here are some simple steps to get you in the end zone:

Christ-confidence comes from having an eternal perspective (not trapped in the immediate). Rom. 8:28 and Phil. 1:6, bam! Nothing can keep you from God's destiny except you! It is a choice.

Living by God's promises (2 Peter 1:4). God's Word will…

- Guide us with wisdom (Ps.119:105)
- Comfort us with understanding (Ps. 119:52)
- Strengthen us with boldness (Rom. 8:37)

No pun intended, but standing on the promises of God creates a firm foundation!
Trusting in our relationship with Jesus (1 John 4:4–5, Jer. 17:7) The result of such a relationship?

- You'll live up to a new level
- You'll train up in the Word

- You'll think up of your destiny

Seems everything hinges on trust and obey. Yea, but so often as soon as the enemy strikes, we turn and run! We have good intentions, but our actions betray our confidence. Listen, get this: those who rise above their circumstances understand that God uses every experience for good (Rom. 8:28). You are always in God's hand. Focusing (eternal perspective) upon his sovereign will and the good he has in store for you is not easy in hard times (ah, trust me on that one). I understand! But I also know that God never allows anything to touch us that he will not turn to our benefit and the good of his kingdom. So grab your helmet and get in the game!

Tackle something big for God today! I will too.

You First
by Coach Rock

There is a Bible principle in Matthew 14 that really needs to be reinstated as an important first step in just about every circumstance of the Christian life. By reinstated I mean, we have been so masterfully manipulated into living our Christian life with the same expectations we have for our government and social values. *Entitlements, baby!* We let government tell us how to live and what to do. In return, we get goodies/something for nothing. It has become the norm in our culture to expect handouts. Let Big Brother take care of you. You don't need to do anything to merit your reward. We actually right now (February 2014) have more people taking entitlements in the US than those who don't. What a sad commentary on this generation of Americans!

This is going to take some effort on my part and about the same by the readership.

Following the miracle of the loaves and the fishes, Jesus instructed his disciples to get into a boat while he went up into a mountain to pray.

No sooner had the disciples begun their voyage on the sea, than a storm arose, causing them to fear for their lives. The Bible says it was the fourth watch, which would be the last watch before daylight, the darkest time of the night. The Lord was aware of their circumstances; Matthew says in verse. 25, "Jesus went unto them, walking on the sea." KJV

When they saw Jesus, the disciples thought they were seeing a spirit; they cried out in fear. Jesus said unto them, "Be of good cheer; it is I; be not afraid" (Matt 14:27, KJV). By the way, notice that in the midst of the raging seas, Jesus makes one heck of a radical statement: "Be of good cheer!" When all chaos has broken loose and you have no answer, grab hold of Jesus and get to celebrate his love and his care over you. Incredibly, Jesus is telling us to not just grab hold of his arm, but demonstrate supernatural trust by cheering during the highest waves!

When Peter saw Jesus walking on the water, he asked the Lord to let him come to him. Jesus said in verse 29, "Come." And Peter stepped out of the boat into the water. Bingo, first step! How 'bout you? Trust him enough to take that first step out of the boat?

There is the first step of salvation. In order to come to Jesus, one must make the first step toward him. Jesus has already taken the first step toward us, the cross proves that. Can I ask you: have you taken that first step? Have you received Christ as your Savior? Jesus said in John 6:37, "All that the Father giveth me shall come to me; and him that cometh to me I will in no wise cast out." KJV

There is the first step of service. When Jesus called the disciples, he called them to serve. When Jesus saved us, he called us to serve. Every church has its number of faithful servants, people who seem to do everything. They can be counted on when something needs to get done.

Again, there are those who would like to serve, but they are fearful. They feel inadequate. They feel like they have no skills or talents, that the Lord would never use them. Nothing could be further from the truth. When you got saved, God equipped you with a spiritual gift. Let me tell you what separates you from serving: one step. You must be willing to take the first step. And in order to ever slay your giant, bring down your wall of Jericho, cross your Red Sea, or follow the call of God: put on the whole armor, get a good wide stance, eyes on the prize and faith to move mountains. One step can change the world.

These next several offerings are from Mark Trotter. He is the teaching pastor at Northwest Bible Church in Hilliard, Ohio. Mark and I both were bookend linebackers at Maranatha Baptist University in the mid-to-late '70s. We were happy to take your head off if you were foolish enough to run between the tackles. He has been in pastoral ministry for thirty-five years and is a very popular speaker. He has a real gift for spelling out Bible doctrine and the harder things of God in easy to understand language, and he throws in his unique storytelling and sense of humor—well, you get one of my favorite speakers and writers on the East Coast.

No More Excuses…Man Up and Play Ball
Read Romans 2:15 and 1 Corinthians 16:13

I was a street-baller as a kid in what would be considered not-the-greatest neighborhood in Miami. A dude two doors down murdered his wife, drug deals were being made on a daily basis (out of my house nonetheless!), and I even witnessed a shooting in my front lawn. Not usually what you think about when someone tells you they're from Miami. And in our hood, we used to love when someone's trash pile included cans of paint. That was when it was time to restripe the imaginary football field we made out of our street. And I mean, we went all out! We had the ten-yard increments perfectly laid out with the one-yard hashmarks in between, and the field crew at Notre Dame would have been impressed with what we had goin' on in each end zone! My knees and elbows still bear the marks of our very unforgiving asphalt field, and I can still make out the scar on my thigh from taking out the neighbor's mailbox. But my first year of organized ball as a freshman let me know that there was a big difference between that brand of football and what I was accustomed to in the street! Playing in the street had taught me aggression and to somehow love the feeling of slamming my body into someone else's with the intent of taking their proverbial head off. But there were two key things I didn't get in the street: one was discipline and the other was taking personal responsibility when things go wrong. Ya see, in the street, it was always someone else's fault. There was always an excuse or someone other than yourself to blame for plays gone bad. That doesn't work real well when you're playing on an actual team—with a real coach! I distinctly remember one night in practice, the coach bustin' my chops (in front of the entire team, mind you!) about the whole "accusing" others and "excusing" myself thing. I'm sure the words he screamed to the top of his lungs that night are still reverberating somewhere in outer space today: "Trotter, no more excuses! Just man up and play ball!" And if you're an athlete, you know just how important of a lesson that is to learn. Sad to say, many athletes have learned that lesson when it comes to the whole world of sports, but have not allowed that lesson to be translated into their own personal life off the field or off the court. As a pastor for the last three and a half decades, you don't know how many times I wish I could have screamed to the top of my lungs to people I've tried to help with their problems, "Stop making excuses! Just man up and play ball!" Listen y'all, somewhere in life we've gotta man up, play the hand we've been dealt, and get on with our life! Romans 2:15 talks about our propensity as humans to spend our lives accusing someone else for our problems or excusing ourselves because of our problems! Again, somewhere along the way, we just have to come to a place of spiritual resolve where we just stop it! But the question is how? May I remind you today, that when we placed our faith in the Lord Jesus Christ and called upon his name to save us, we became a partaker of his very own divine nature because the Holy Spirit of God took up residence inside of us! The biblical reality is we're not who we used to be! He's made us new creatures in Christ (2 Corinthians 5:17), and we have a different power now working on the inside of us! And with that in mind, there's a little four-word admonition that God gives us through the apostle Paul in 1 Corinthians 16:13 that I think can help all of us as we seek to stop the accusing and excusing. Paul says, "Quit you like men." In the context of the entire book of 1 Corinthians, let me tell you what he means by that little statement—because it's monumental! God is saying to us, "Stop living like the natural man you were! And start living like the supernatural man you are!" The way we might say it today is, "Man up! And start living out who you are in Christ!" Ya see, y'all, we only get one shot at this whole life thing! We get one shot to make a difference, one shot to do what God left us here to do, one shot to fulfill his purpose for our lives, one shot to invest in eternity! And the fact is, if we spend our time accusing and excusing, we're gonna blow our shot, we're gonna miss our chance, we're gonna squander our opportunity! And we've gotta realize that while we're spending our time accusing and excusing, the world's still spinning, the clock's still ticking, the game's still being played, the war's still raging, the battle's still being fought—and with every second we delay, more and more people on this planet drop off into a Godless, Christless eternity in hell! Simply put, if we're busying ourselves pointing fingers, we won't be busying ourselves pointing people to Christ! Ya know, the more I think about it, that night at practice, my coach wasn't too far from giving me some of the best biblical advice I would ever receive. May the simple truth of 1 Corinthians 16:13 that he unwittingly paraphrased that night reverberate in our heads and our hearts for the rest of our lives: "No more excuses! Just man up and play ball!"

The Devil's Playbook Only Has Three Plays!

Read 1 John 2:15–16 and Eph 6:10–17 before continuing. We were playing our cross-town rival my sophomore year in high school. Both teams scored on the opening drive, but after that, we were pretty much limited to our own side of the field as were they. Neither team could sustain a drive, and I remember the coaches being absolutely livid at half-time. But as we came out in the third quarter, it was just a whole lot more of the same for both teams. A first down here and there, only to have to punt it away— and that was pretty much the name of the ball-game all the way until the final minutes of the fourth quarter. With about three and a half minutes remaining in the game, they punted to us, and we began what would be our final drive of the game from about our own 30. The play the coach called was a very simple, no frills, 14 dive—a play designed to be run right up the gut and right off of my butt at the right guard position. The right tackle and I fired off the ball, the running back hit the hole, and we picked up about four yards. The next play the coach called was a 14 dive and went for six yards and a first down. He sent in the next play, and you guessed it, another 14 dive that went for another five yards. And no exaggeration, every single play in that entire drive was a 14 dive! We were able to score and win the game, running the same exact play on every single down, with the defense knowing full well what the next play was going to be!

That series of downs and play-calling from our coach has served as a constant reminder to me through the years of the devil's strategy against us. Ya see, the devil is like a coach with only three plays in his entire playbook. They're identified for us in 1 John 2:15, as "The lust of the flesh, the lust of the eyes, and the pride of life." (KJV) I mean, that's it! That's all he's got to work with. Oh, sure, he runs 'em out of a lot of different sets and formations, with a lot of motion to mask what he's doing, but when it's all said and done and the fat lady is startin' to do her thing, it's all just three plays! And I ask you, what coach in his right mind would have the audacity to only include three plays in his playbook and expect to win games? And yet ya know what's crazy? The devil's been running his three plays ever since Genesis 3:6, and generation after generation and individual after individual continues to get smashed in the mouth by his offense, as if we were clueless about what to expect! Listen, y'all, sure, the devil runs a powerhouse offense, but one thing it isn't—it isn't sophisticated! As I like to say, "It's not rocket surgery, folks! (mixed metaphor intended!)" It's time we woke up and allowed the Spirit of God who lives in us to give us the discernment to read the devil's play and stand in the Lord's strength and power against him!

> And when the woman saw that the tree was good for food (lust of the flesh), and that it was pleasant to the eyes (lust of the eyes), and a tree to be desired to make one wise (pride of life), she took of the fruit thereof, and did eat, and gave also unto her husband with her; and he did eat.
>
> Genesis 3:6, KJV

It's All about the Shoes!

Read Ephesians 6:10–17. It was my first time to play in the Orange Bowl. Wow! Me—playing in a stadium with a seating capacity of over 80,000! I had watched the Hurricanes and the Dolphins play there numerous times as a kid growing up in Miami, and now it was my turn. But it's not what you're thinking. I was still playing high school ball, and the stadium that night may (emphasis on "may!") have been filled to a whopping 5 percent of its capacity. But the whole Orange Bowl thing was still a pretty big deal for a kid from Miami, especially for those of us from the other side of the tracks. Pulling up in the buses that night to this legendary stadium and swaggin' into the same locker room where Bob Griese, Larry Cszonka, and Paul Warfield would be doing their thing on Sunday was just crazy cool to me. I can assure ya, I felt a whole lot badder than I was! We had to get to the stadium earlier than a typical game that night because with the newly installed artificial turf, the cleats we normally wore weren't permitted. There had been a lot of hype in the media about major problems players were having trying to keep their footing on the turf, especially in the rain, so the Orange Bowl was allowing players to borrow shoes specifically designed to address the slipping issue when playing in their stadium. In the locker room, they kind of had it set up like when you go up to the counter and check out shoes at a bowling alley. So I go up to the window and tell the dude my size. He hands the shoes to me, and as I'm walking back to my locker looking down at them, I was thinking to myself, *Ain't no way I'm wearing these suckers out there!* Man, I wish you could've seen those babies! They looked to me like corrective shoes with about 1,000 tiny little rubber spikes on the bottom. Yeah, I get it—the manufacturer was concentrating on some kind of design to fix the traction issue, but it was more than apparent that there was one thing nobody in that design department was thinking about, and that's what in the heck they looked like! For real, you talk about a nasty-looking shoe! I may have been from the other side of the tracks, but I wasn't clueless about style! And my philosophy was, if you're gonna be doin' something cool, you might as well look cool doin' it! So as I'm making my way back to my locker working through this whole nasty shoe gig, all of a sudden, I had an incredible idea! I had my brand-new (and way cool!) orange high-top Chuck Taylor All-Star tennis shoes in my bag, and I started thinking how cool it would be to run out of the tunnel at game time sportin' Chuck's! And they'd be perfect with our orange, black, and white unis! But the question would be, would they give me the traction I needed? So during warm-ups, I gave it a shot, and I couldn't believe it: they were perfect! Since I was playing right guard on the offensive line, I tested every assignment I knew I would have to be absolutely sure they were gonna work. I tested firing off the ball out of my stance and couldn't believe how they seemed to grip the turf. I tested pulling and felt like I was able to turn on a dime. I tested pass blocking, and again, felt like I was able to plant my feet and explode up into the defensive lineman. I was stoked! I wondered why others hadn't already tried wearing the Chuck's—especially looking as smooth as I did! The game started, and man, it was a dog fight. I finally settled into the game, no longer thinking about the cool venue—not to mention how cool I must've looked to all my homies in the stands. We went into halftime with the score tied at 0-0. We had two incredible drives into the red zone in the first half, but had come away empty both times because the same running back fumbled—inside the five yard-line, I might add! Grrrrr! (You might have to be or have been an offensive lineman to understand the weight behind that "Grrrrr!")

As we came out in the second half, they kicked the ball to us, and we started the first drive of the third quarter from our own 20. We were moving the ball well and had strung together several first downs, bringing us into their territory on about the 40. As we were in the huddle, I heard the tap of several pretty major raindrops on the top of my helmet, and by the time we were actually running the play, the bottom had dropped out! One of those tropical Miami rainstorms that seem to pop up out of nowhere had unleashed itself right over the stadium with such force, the field couldn't drain the water off fast enough. I could tell on that play that I had lost quite a bit of traction and was thinking to myself, *Oh, crap!* And wouldn't ya know, when the halfback came into the huddle with the next play from the sideline, it was a 14 dive! A play totally dependent upon me firing off of the ball and getting into the body of the defensive lineman or linebacker. Usually, my favorite play. Usually! We broke out of the huddle, the quarterback started the count, the rain pounding like crazy, and I could tell as I was getting down into my stance—I had nothin'! Absolutely no traction whatsoever! The center snapped the ball, and that defensive lineman was all up in my stuff in a fraction of a second, pushing me backward like I was on a pair of ice skates in an ice skating rink! He dropped the running back like a rag doll for a three yard loss. I immediately ran to the sideline calling for my backup, frantically trying to find somebody with a size 11 shoe who wasn't going to be getting into the game to trade shoes with. So much for cool shoes. 'Cuz if you're an offensive lineman, ain't too many things more uncool than getting your behind pushed into your own backfield and your guy dropping the ball carrier for a loss—no matter how cool your shoes are! I mean, that's about as bad as a running back fumbling inside the five yard line! I finally found somebody to trade shoes with, and I can tell ya this, when I ran back onto the field, I didn't give a rip about what stadium I was in or what my shoes looked like—all I was concerned with was having something on my feet that would allow me to stand my ground against the opposition and allow me to fulfill my assignment! And ya know what? That whole ordeal in the Orange Bowl that night taught me an invaluable lesson about the Christian life. 'Cuz the fact is, if we're gonna stand our ground against the opposition (Satan and all of his highly regimented network of demonic forces and powers (Ephesians 6:12)), and if we're gonna fulfill our assignment on the earth, it is totally dependent upon whether or not we have on the right kind of shoes! Yes, shoes!

Ya see, biblically speaking, one of the most important parts of our uniform (armor), and yet probably one of the least talked about is the shoes we wear. It shakes out like this. Our Creator knows the adversity we're gonna face in the game of life, and with that in mind, he has specifically designed shoes that will keep us standing when the wind blows, the rain pounds, the ground beneath us is slippery, and the enemy is trying to get all up in our stuff. According to Ephesians 6:15, they're called the gospel shoes. And no, they're probably not what most of the people in the stands are gonna think are cool, but, buddy, they'll keep the enemy from knocking you on your keister and will allow you to carry out your kingdom assignment!

Ephesians 6:15 explains that what these shoes actually are is our constant spiritual awareness of the eternal destiny of the people all around us every day, along with our constant willingness and readiness to proclaim to them the message that freed us from our sin, and allowed us to enter into an eternal, personal, intimate love relationship with the God of the universe. So many Christians wonder why they can be so diligent to get into the truth of God's Word (Eph. 6:14a); seek to live a righteous life (Eph. 6:14b); express faith in Christ (Eph. 6:16); think like someone who possesses salvation (Eph. 6:17); and yet, still not be able to stand in the victory our Lord Jesus Christ has already provided for us (Eph. 6:11, 13, 14a). According to Ephesians 6:15, it's for the very simple reason that we don't have our gospel shoes on! And without 'em, the enemy has the ability to push us around like we're on a pair of ice skates on an ice skating rink and knock us off of our spiritual feet at virtually any moment. Oh, may God help us to see that sharing the gospel isn't what super-Christians do to be spiritual. It's what normal Christians do for survival! Listen, y'all, the third quarter is about to begin, and the forecast calls for severe storms. Let's take off our cool Chuck Taylor's and get our gospel shoes on, so we can stand our ground against the opposition and fulfill our kingdom assignment!

Cry a River. Build a Bridge, and Get Over It!
Read Philippians 3:13–14

I had finally come back to my old stompin' grounds. I had gone off to college, met the babe of my dreams (and beyond my dreams!), had gotten married, and was pastoring singles in southern California. I hadn't been back to Miami since I graduated from high school. God had done so many things in my life in that six-year period I was away. It was cool to be back and reflect on days gone by and be able to rejoice in the victories God had graciously given to me. Ya see, not all the memories were good. Like most of us did, I grew up in a home that was whack. I think the politically correct way of saying it is a dysfunctional home, but if you've lived through it, you know that the word *whack* is a much more graphic and realistic word. But as I'm cruisin' down the road thinking back on all this stuff, coincidentally enough, I got behind a car that was sportin' a bumper sticker that seemed to put into words the very message I felt the Lord had brought me back home to get. The bumper sticker simply said, "Cry a river. Build a bridge.

And get over it." And ya know what I've found in seeking to help countless numbers of people through the years? We all have an "it" that we need to "get over!" Sad, but unbelievably true. And I've gotta tell ya—few people I've met have actually allowed God's grace to get them over their it. And oh my, I've heard some horrific its through the years. After hearing so many of 'em, you start to see that they all seem to fall into a certain pattern or theme.

"My dad was in idiot."
"My dad left us."
"My dad was a pervert."
"My dad never came to my games."
"My dad never told me he loved me."
"My dad worked all the time."
"My dad beat me."

"My dad beat my mom."
>   Or
"My mom was overbearing."
"My mom was dominant in our family."
"My mom was a tramp."
"My mom had multiple affairs."
"My mom was depressed all the time."
"My mom was addicted to prescription drugs."
"My mom abandoned us."
>   Or
"I grew up on the other side of the tracks."
"I grew up wearing hand-me-downs."
"I grew up poor."
"I was abused."
"I had a tough life."

And oh my, all of that stuff is very real—and very sad! After hearing many people's story, I find myself thanking God for the cush life I didn't realize I actually had! But as horrific as all of that stuff in our past may have been, if we have the Lord Jesus Christ living in us by his Spirit, there comes a point in time when we must purposely choose to allow the Lord to help us get over it! Listen, if you're still letting your old man control you by your bitterness toward him, if you're still blaming your momma, if you're still looking backward, if you're still bringing the past into your present, if you're still making excuses by accusing someone else or something else, cry a river. Build a bridge. And get over it! Okay, so your dad was an idiot, your mom was a mental case, or however you chose to describe 'em. Forgive 'em! Pack it in, man, and get on with your life! Sure, cry a river one final time if you feel the need, and the reality is, that may very well be something you need to do! Yeah, I know it hurt you, it was excruciating for you, it was unbelievably traumatic and horrific, and believe me, I am so, so sorry you had to go through it! So yeah, man, I get it, you may need to cry a river one last time. But then, after you do, by God's grace and power, recognize that it's time to build a bridge! Find a spiritual mentor who can help you, first of all, to build into your life some of the fundamental pillars of truth (1 Timothy 3:15) from the Word of God. And secondly, help you to get yourself established in who you are in Christ and allow those spiritual realities to be the bridge God uses to help you to get over your it! Regardless of what it is! And once you get over the bridge, don't go back to the other side! Make Paul's declaration in Philippians 3:13–14, the war cry of your life—for the rest of your life.

> Brethren, I count not myself to have apprehended: but this one thing I do, forgetting those things which are behind, and reaching forth unto those things which are before, I press toward the mark for the prize of the high calling of God in Christ Jesus.
>
> Philippians 3:13–14

Samson: The Strongest Man in the World! Or Samson: The Weakest Man in the World
Read Judges 13–16

God had an unbelievable plan for how he wanted to use a man in the Old Testament by the name of Samson. The tragedy is, however, Samson cashed it in because he had a major case of the heebee-jeebies for a foreign woman. I'm not sure what you already know about Samson, but on one hand, we could refer to him as "the *strongest* man who ever lived," and yet on the other hand, we could refer to him as "the *weakest* man who ever lived!" Listen, from a physical standpoint, this dude had the strength of a fictitious superhero like Superman or the Incredible Hulk, but from a spiritual standpoint, he couldn't even muster the simple strength to tell his flesh "no!" He had the power to conquer every man on earth—except one, *himself*! And what we learn from

Judges 13–16 is that Samson was a guy that had everything in the world going for him! God had literally stacked the deck for him. Or if you don't mind me mixing the metaphors, God put him up to bat in the bottom of the ninth with bases loaded and told him to swing for the fence! And he squandered it all because rather than serve God's purposes for his life, he chose to serve himself! Rather than becoming a champion for God, he became a selfish, self-willed, self-absorbed, self-seeking, self-gratifying, self-loving, self-monger! And while we're on this *self* thing, may I remind you that God tells us in 2 Timothy 3:1–2, that the number 1 characteristic that makes these last days so incredibly perilous is that we are lovers of our own *selves*! Perhaps, then, there just might be some things we can learn from Samson's life that can help us!

Let's give it a shot. Notice:

1. Samson was the product of a supernatural birth. Judges 13:2 lets us know that his mother was barren and had absolutely no hope of bearing a child apart from the supernatural working of the angel of the Lord (an Old Testament appearance of our Lord Jesus Christ!), who appears to her in verse 3, and causes her to be able to conceive and bear Samson.
2. Samson had the privilege of being set apart for the Lord's service from his very birth. Judges 13:5 says, "For the child shall be a Nazarite unto god from the womb."(kjv) Ya see, that's what a Nazarite was "one who was sanctified or set apart for the Lord's service."
3. Samson possessed the power of the very Holy Spirit of God upon his life. Judges 13:25 says that Samson was moved by the Spirit of the Lord. Judges 14:5–6 says he was empowered mightily by the Spirit of the Lord upon him to overcome a roaring lion! And Judges 15:14–16 says

he was empowered by the Spirit of the Lord to overcome his enemies— a thousand of 'em at one time!

4. Samson was provided a *beginning* that was filled with unending promise and potential. The last part of Judges 13:5 says, "And he shall begin to deliver Israel out of the hand of the Philistines." (KJV) And I want you to notice that what Samson did with the *beginning* God gave to him was limited only by Samson's own choices and his willingness to be surrendered to God's plans and purposes for him. And yet with all of these incredible realities and this unending potential in his life, because of pride, self-will, selfish ambition, and allowing himself to think with the wrong part of his anatomy, he forfeited the real impact God could have used him to have, and he squandered the potential glory he could have brought to the Lord through his life.

He becomes for us, the classic biblical example of a *wasted life*! And lest all of that sound like a bunch of spiritual verbiage and worthless facts about a dude who lived several thousand years ago, let me tell ya why I took the time to go into those four key things about Samson's life that I listed above. It's because Samson's story is unbelievably similar to ours! Because check this out, for all of us who know the Lord Jesus Christ as our savior, just like Samson:

1. We too were the product of a supernatural birth. No, not a physical one like Samson— but a supernatural spiritual birth that we call salvation or being born again! Ephesians 2:12–13 says we were without hope until the angel of the Lord, the Lord Jesus Christ, supernaturally drew us to himself. And 1 Peter 1:23 says that we were "born again, not of corruptible seed (physical seed/birth), but of incorruptible, by the word of God, which liveth and abideth forever."

2. We too were given the privilege of being set apart for the Lord's service from our very birth. And of course, that would be referring again to our spiritual birth! 1 Corinthians 6:11 tells us that when the Holy Spirit of God washed us in Christ's blood and we received our justification or our salvation in Christ, that at that very moment, we were sanctified or set apart by the Holy Spirit of God for the Lord's service.
3. We too possess the power of the very Holy Spirit of God upon our lives. Acts 17:2 says that, "In him we live and move, and have our being." (kjv) 2 Corinthians 6:16 says that in us, he lives and moves and has his being! And 1 Peter 5:8 tells us that though our enemy (or adversary) walks about like a roaring lion, 1 John 4:4 says that we have been given the power by the one who lives in us to overcome him! And not just him, but the enemy of sin that resides in the members of our body. Romans 6:13–14 says that through God's power in us, the enemy of sin no longer has dominion (or power) over us!
4. We too have been provided a beginning that is filled with unending promise and potential. 2 Corinthians 5:17 says that now that we are in Christ, we are new creatures, and that "old things are passed away; behold, all things are become new!" Listen, that's the beginning God gave to all of us! And just like in Samson's case, what we do with the beginning God gave to us is limited only by our own choices and our willingness to be surrendered to God's plans and purposes through us!

Do you see that unbelievable connection we have with Samson? We, too, are men who have everything in the world going for us! God has literally stacked the deck for us! God has put us up to bat in the bottom of the ninth with bases loaded and has told us to swing for the fence! And yet the absolute tragedy and travesty is men who have actually experienced a supernatural spiritual birth, men who have been set apart by that spiritual birth for the Lord's service, men empowered by God's own holy spirit in them, and men granted the unbelievable privilege and promise of a brand-new beginning with unlimited potential to bring God glory, just like Samson, forfeit the real impact God intends for their lives. And just like Samson, they squander their potential to glorify God, and their ultimate accounting at the judgment seat of Christ will reveal that for all intents and purposes, they wasted their life! Oh, for God's glory's sake, may that not be me…and may it not be you! May we learn from the negative example of Samson to keep ourselves off the path of self-love and self-destruction and fulfill God's glorious purpose for our lives!

Which Direction Are Your Feet Pointing?
Read Proverbs 4:26; Psalm 119:59

We've seen from Judges 13–16 that the way God positioned Samson to use his life to glorify him is strikingly similar to the way God has positioned us. He is the classic biblical example of a man with incredible privilege and promise, who forfeited God's purposes, squandered his potential, caused the enemies of God to blaspheme his holy and worthy name, and epitomizes the tragedy of a wasted life. How the whole section in Scripture covering Samson's life ends is very telling. Because you know where we actually find Samson in Judges 16:29–31? He's buried beneath the rubble of his own self-destruction and his brothers have come to pull him out of it to at least give him a decent burial. Check it out in these verses:

> And Samson took hold of the two middle pillars upon which the house stood, and on which it was borne up, of the one with his right hand, and of the other with his left. And Samson said, 'Let me die with the Philistines.' And

he bowed himself with all his might; and the house fell upon the lords, and upon all the people that were therein. So the dead which he slew at his death were more than they which he slew in his life. Then his brethren and all the house of his father came down, and took him, and brought him up, and buried him between Zorah and Eshtaol in the burying place of Manoah his father. And he judged Israel twenty years.

Judges 16:29, KJV

And I want you to notice the last sentence in this section. The end of verse 31 says, "And he judged Israel twenty years." (Judges 16:29, KJV) Listen y'all, he had a twenty-year shot to do what God had created him to do, and would you look at him lying there beneath the rubble of devastation and destruction? And again I remind you, all self-inflicted! And ya know how he got there? The same exact way that men end up there in the twenty-first century!

And it's the key principle I'd like for us to see. *Where we end up in life is determined by the direction of our feet.* As I've said before, that's not rocket surgery, folks! I mean, in terms of learning to walk, that principle almost seems to be innate! Even a toddler knows that if you're facing in one direction and you want to go in another, you've gotta turn and get your feet pointed in that direction! And you would think that that principle would be innate in Christians in terms of our "walk," but for some strange reason, I can assure you, it isn't! And maybe that's why God just flat out commands us in Proverbs 4:26 to "ponder the path of our feet!" He's saying to us, pay careful attention to the direction your feet are pointing and ponder that path. In other words, look down that path about twenty years or so because that's where we're gonna end up! And if we can't figure out just where that path actually leads, all we really have to do is look at where that path has taken others who had their feet pointed in that direction because that's exactly where it will take us! And I'd like for you to look with me at what the Scripture reveals about Samson's path and the direction of his feet. Notice that Judges 14:1 says, "And Samson went DOWN to Timnath, and saw a woman in Timnath of the daughters of the Philistines." (KJV) And sure, I get it, geographically, Timnath was at a lower elevation. But if you check the context, it wasn't just "geographical." It was also a *downward* direction for his spiritual life! Look with me at the first part of Judges 14:5. It says, "Then Samson went *down*." Let's just stop there for a second. What you'll notice in this verse and what you'll notice as you read and reread Judges 13–16 is that virtually every decision Samson makes sends him spiritually in a *downward* direction! Judges 16:1 says, "Then went Samson to Gaza, and saw there an harlot, and went in unto her." (KJV) Now obviously, that was a *downward* move spiritually, even though the verse doesn't actually say he went *down* to Gaza. But what the passage does tell us is that when his brothers came to remove his dead body out of the rubble, verse 31 says they "came *down*, and took him, and brought him *up*." Do you see it? These were all *downward* spiritual moves that proved to be the demise of Samson over this twenty-year period of his life. It makes me wonder how the story of our lives might read if God were to record it twenty years from now. Maybe it might read like this: "And he went *down* the hall to talk to one of his female coworkers." Or "He went *down* to his old hang-out to watch the game with his buddies." Or "He went *downstairs*," or "He went *down* to the basement to check his e-mail or to search the Internet" or "He scrolled *down* on Facebook to the profile of his old girlfriend." Or "He *downloaded* pictures from a pornographic Web site." Or it could be a thousand different *downward* moves that we're capable of making spiritually! I don't know how it might read, but I do know this, as some of us are reading this today, our feet are pointing spiritually in a direction, which unless something happens, will prove to be our *downfall*! And again, unless something happens, some of our brothers will have to come *down* to where we've allowed ourselves to get and lift us *up* out of the rubble of our own self-destruction. It may be a year from now... five years...ten years...or twenty. And know this—it will be such a travesty! Because God destined and predestined us for so much more and powered and empowered us for so much more! Listen, if some of us could actually see the direction our feet are pointing and where that path will take us twenty years from now, this would be a monumental day in our life, because this would be the day we turned our feet in a different direction! We would turn our feet from that path that today looks and feels so inviting, fun, and fulfilling, but will ultimately be our spiritual unraveling. Oh, may the decision David made in Psalm 119:59 be the decision we choose to make today. David said, "I thought on my ways, and *turned my feet* unto thy testimonies." (KJV) I can assure you of this— if we make "that" decision today, twenty years from today, we'll be overjoyed we did!

Where Will You Be Twenty Years from Now?
Read Ps. 119:47–48, 97, 113, 127–128, 140, 159, 163, 165–167

Samson was a stud. Physically, that is! Spiritually, he was nothing but an absolute wimp—just a carnal, self-absorbed, worthless chump. The Lord had set the dude up with unending promise and potential to make an impact on this planet for God's glory and kingdom, and yet over a twenty-year span, his feet continuously led him in a *downward* direction. Oh, that Samson would have come to the place of resolve that David did in Psalm 119:59! David said, "I thought on my ways and *turned my feet* unto Thy testimonies." (KJV) And I say to you today—oh, that you and I would likewise come to that monumental place of resolve! Because here's the deal, y'all, *the real determining factor of where your steps take you in the next twenty years will be based on where you choose to place the Word of God on a daily basis.* And when I'm talking about "where you choose to place the Word of God in your life," I'm talking about several things:

I'm talking about your *attitude* toward it—where you place it in your *mind*.

I'm talking about your *belief and trust* in it—where you place it in your *heart*.

I'm talking about your *surrender* to it—where you place it in your *will*.

Do you think you get that? Let me rephrase my point, even if it's for nothing other than emphasis! *The thing that will determine where your life will be twenty years from now is where you choose to place the Word of God in your life and what you choose to do with it on a daily basis.* Could I be just flat out honest with ya? Most men never seem to get that!

They're too *married to their job*.

They're too *enamored with sports*.

They're too *preoccupied with lust*.

They're too *consumed with money* (and the *things* money can buy)—to ever really allow the Word of God to have the place of preeminence it deserves in their life!

Do you realize the Bible is our life line to God—and our *only* life line to God? Sure, if you've been born again, I know you have the Holy Spirit of God living inside of you, but the Spirit of God *always, always, always* works in conjunction with the Word of God! In fact, that's one of the key reasons the Spirit of God took up residence in you—to teach you the Bible, because we can't learn it without him (1 John 2:27). And yet the sad reality is—most men spend more time doing their *hobby* over the course of a week (balling, golfing, bowling, skiing, weightlifting, or whatever else-ing!) than they spend in the Word of God. Most men spend more time *feeding their face* in the course of a week, than they spend *feeding their soul* the Truth of God. Most men spend more time reading page after page of *sports articles* over the course of a week than they spend in the pages of the Word of God. Most men spend more time on *Facebook* in the course of a week, than they spend on their *face* in God's *book*. Most men spend more time *lusting on women* in the course of a week than they spend *longing for god* through the pages of his book.

And just so we don't forget, let me say it yet again, "*The* determining factor of where we'll be twenty years from now is what we do with the Word of God!" Our problem in the twenty-first century is this: most men never learn what it is to *love* the Word of God. Ten times in Psalm 119 alone, David talked about his *love* for God's Word (Ps. 119:47–48, 97, 113, 127–128, 140, 159, 163, 165–167). I ask you, where are the men in the twenty-first century who genuinely *love* the Word of God? Do you?

Most men never learn what it is to *feast* on the Word of God. Jeremiah said in Jeremiah 15:16, "Thy words were found, and I did *eat* them; and thy word was unto me the joy and rejoicing of mine heart." (KJV) I ask you, where are the men in the twenty-first century who know what it is to *feast* on God's Word? Do you? Most men would rather have *physical food* in their stomach than *spiritual food* in their soul. In Job 23:12, Job said, "Neither have I gone back from the commandment of his lips; I have esteemed the words of his mouth more than my necessary food." (KJV) And oh, I ask you, where are the men in the twenty-first century that would pass up a meal because of their hunger for the Word of God? Would you? Most men never come to the place of *reverencing* the Word of God. In Ezra 9:4, Ezra said, "Then were assembled unto me every one that *trembled* at the words of the God of Israel." (KJV) And once again I ask you, where are the men in the twenty-first century who so *revere* the Word of God that they can even comprehend the concept of actually *trembling* at it? Can you? And I realize this is some pretty sobering stuff. My goal in bringing it up, though, certainly isn't an attempt to make any of us feel bad or put any of us on a guilt trip. My intent is to allow the Word of God to pierce our hearts, to bring us to a place of resolve when it comes to the Word of God, that motivates us into action! I ask you today, do you sense the Holy Spirit of God stirring in your heart about the place the Word of God has had in your life? Is he motivating you into action when it comes to his Word? Then, will you say these four simple yet monumental things to the Lord today?

1. "Lord, by Your grace, and by the power of Your Spirit within me, I determine today to *turn my feet* toward the Word of God everyday for the next year" (Psalm 119:59, KJV).
2. "Lord, by Your grace, and by the power of Your Spirit within me, I determine to *seek you* with all of my heart through the pages of Your Word" (Deut. 4:29, KJV).
3. "Lord, by Your grace, and by the power of Your Spirit within me, I determine to *learn* what it is to *love* the Word of God, and to *tremble* at Your Words" (Psalm 119:47–48; Ezra 9:4, KJV).
4. "Lord, by Your grace, and by the power of Your Spirit within me, I determine to *surrender* to You anything and everything You reveal to me through Your Word that needs to be *changed* in my life" (Psalm 119:48, KJV).

Listen, if you can honestly say those four things to God today and will allow him to perfect them in your life over the course of the next twenty years, I will assure ya, you'll be a major player in God's kingdom! And you will never, ever, ever regret that decision for all of eternity!

Your Domino—and Your Domino Trail
Read 2 Timothy 4:7; Acts 13:25; 20:24

Did you ever play with dominoes when you were a kid? Remember how we'd spend an hour or more setting 'em up in all kinds of crazy and extravagant configurations, just to be able to tip one of 'em so we could have the twenty to thirty seconds of fun watching them fall over? Actually, that's what I thought dominoes were for! I was an adult before I knew that dominoes was actually a game, and all of those dots were part of what was involved in playing it. I just thought they were to make the little squares look cool when they were falling over! And I bring the whole domino thing up to illustrate a key life principle. It is extremely important to understand that God has an incredible "domino trail" set up for you! Your domino trail is his plan for your life. And it is a very strategic, well-thought-out. and specific course. Biblically, it is very uniquely "your course" (2 Timothy 4:7; Acts 13:25; 20:24). That is, it is specific to you. And by the time you get to the end of it, it is designed to bring you *exponential blessing*! Not necessarily a cush life, but definitely a *life that matters*! But it is also extremely important to understand that the devil also has an incredible domino trail set up for you! And it, too, is a very strategic, well-thought-out, and specific course. Biblically, it is referred to as "the course of this world" (Eph. 2:2). And by the time you get to the end of it, it is designed to bring you *exponential pain* and *heartache*. His course is the epitome of a *wasted life*! And what sets each of these domino trails in motion is your domino. Your domino is your *will*—which is expressed through the *choices* you make. The bottom line is, the choices you make in life determine your domino trail. And what both history and the Bible are very clear about is that what you do with your domino matters! Let me share with you three quick things to file somewhere in the very forefront of your thinking about the choices you make.

1. Your choices *matter!* In fact, they matter *a lot*! Not only do they *describe* you—in time, they begin to *define* you!
2. Your choices have *consequences*! They will either have *positive* consequences or they'll have *negative* consequences—but they *always* have consequences! You determine whether

they will be *positive or negative* by which direction you choose to tip your domino.
3. Your choices determine direction and destiny! The fact is, you're gonna *end up* somewhere in life. Where you end up is anything but random though! When it's all said and done, you will have gotten there by the choices you made—or to keep it with our illustration by the direction you chose to tip your domino.

We now have 6,000 years of human history behind us, along with the record of God's holy and inspired Word to help us interpret it. So we now have the luxury of seeing what actually happens to people who tip their domino toward God's course for their lives and what happens to people who tip their domino toward the devil's course or the course of this world. And what history and the Bible reveal to us is that once your dominoes begin to fall in either direction, they begin to take on a life of their own. Just as one domino falls into another that falls into another that falls into another—one good decision falls into another good decision, which falls into another good decision, and in time, those good decisions begin to take on a life of their own. They become the norm in your life. But also realize, that one bad decision falls into another bad decision, which falls into another bad decision, and before you know it, they, too, take on a life of their own. And they too become the norm in your life. Listen now. All of us, regardless of how old we are or what stage of life we're in, are being faced with choices and decisions that are more important and far-reaching than we probably ever realized. My hope through this devotion is that it might serve to be, if nothing else, a *pause* button in your life that will allow you to consider which direction you're presently tipping your dominoes. I ask you to soberly consider what decision, what choice you need to make today to be able to get to the end of your domino trail and be able to say with Paul, "I have fought a good fight, I have finished my course, I have kept the faith: Henceforth there is laid up for me a crown of righteousness, which the Lord, the righteous judge, shall give me at that day: and not to me only, but unto all them also that love His appearing" (2 Timothy 4:7–8, KJV).

And may I remind you:

1. The choice you will make today *matters*.
2. The choice you make today will have *consequences*.
3. The choice you make today will determine *direction and destiny*.

Choose wisely!

What Would You Pay for an Evening with a Hot Babe?
Read 2 Samuel 11

As most locker rooms will reveal, sexual sin is rampant in the twenty-first century! But ya know what's worse? Sexual sin among believers in the twenty-first century is just as rampant! And it's not that we can plead ignorance! I mean, God has been anything but silent on the subject and anything but unclear! In the New Testament, God gives us at least seven major admonitions concerning fornication, which is "sexual sin of any kind." God tells us:

1. Abstain from it! (1 Thess. 4:3)
2. Avoid it! (1 Cor. 7:2)
3. Don't commit it! (1 Cor. 10:8)
4. Kill it or mortify it! (Col. 3:5)
5. Don't let it once be named among you! (Eph. 5:3)
6. Don't company (hang out) with professing Christians who practice it! (2 Cor. 5:11)
7. Flee it! (1 Cor. 6:18)

Wow! Can you think of any other sin the New Testament talks about that brings with it that kind of passion and force? And yet it's crazy, even with all of those powerful admonitions from the God we claim to know and love, somehow at the height and euphoria of temptation—God's voice on the subject can fade into total oblivion. Kind of like the *SERVPRO* commercials: "Like it never even happened!" And as we address the subject, I don't think it's wise for any of us to think that we're not capable of committing this sin—and at virtually any time! What God has used to keep me very humble and dependent in this area is the fact that it happened to David—the only man the Bible ever refers to as a "man after God's own heart." Something tells me that if it happened to David, it could certainly happen to me, and it could certainly happen to you! And if that be true, how could we and how should we defend ourselves against it? Well, let me assure you of this: the time to think about defending ourselves is *now*. It's certainly not, as I've already mentioned, at the height and euphoria of temptation! And if you don't understand that terminology, let me break it down a little further. It ain't when you're alone with some hot babe with a major case of the heebie-jeebies! You got that? No, again, the time to defend ourselves against it is when we're able to think with the part of our anatomy God intended to be used for rational and biblical thinking! And with that in mind, let me share with you four things our flesh will convince us of in the euphoria of temptation.

1. "I can sin and get away with it." Our flesh tells us that, but Numbers 32:23 tells us we can't! It tells us, "And be sure your sin will find you out." (KJV)
2. "I won't reap what I'm sowing." Our flesh tells us that, but Galatians 6:7–8 tells us we will! It tells us, "Be not deceived; God is not mocked: for whatsoever a man soweth, that shall he also reap. For he that soweth to his flesh shall of

the flesh reap corruption; but he that soweth to the Spirit shall of the Spirit reap life everlasting." (KJV)
3. "I can play with fire and not get burned." Our flesh tells us that, but Proverbs 6:27–29 tells us we can't! It tells us, "Can a man take fire in his bosom, and his clothes not be burned? Can one go upon hot coals, and his feet not be burned? So he that goeth in to his neighbour's wife; whosoever toucheth her shall not be innocent." (KJV)
4. "The choices I make today won't have consequences tomorrow." Our flesh tells us that, but both the Bible and history tell us they will! Consider with me the consequences of sexual sin in David's life. I can assure you, if David would have known what that momentary pleasure with that hot babe would ultimately cost him, there isn't a snowball's chance in Hades the dude would have gone for it—I don't care how hot she was! I ask you.

- Would you enter into sexual sin if you knew it would cost you the life of four of your children?
- Would you enter into sexual sin if you knew that the death of three out of the four children would be by murder?
- Would you enter into sexual sin if you knew that the lust you couldn't control would come with a vengeance in one of your sons, that would result in him raping your daughter and his half sister?
- Would you enter into sexual sin if you knew that another one of your sons would be such a sexual fiend that he would literally use a thousand women sexually?

Listen, that was what David paid for his evening with a hot babe! And I'm not suggesting that should we likewise fail in this area, that our consequences would be these, or as severe as these. What I am saying, however, is that if we knew the consequences of our sin before we committed it, it would be enough to deter us—heebie-jeebies or not! So what's the game plan for defending ourselves against the powerful offense of sexual sin? It's really a very simple one.

1. Know the *commands*. I listed seven New Testament commands at the beginning. Know them—even commit them to memory!
2. Consider the *consequences*. Knowing that if you could see what the consequences of the sin would actually be, you would do just what 1 Corinthians 6:18 says to do: "Flee it!"

May God help us to do what our coaches always taught us: *Stick with the game plan!*

Where You at, Man?
Read Genesis 3:1–12

So let's say you're gonna get in your ride and take a trip to see me in Ohio. You pull out your device to the map app, and what's the first thing you've gotta determine? Not where I am, but what? Where you are! Would you mind me asking you today, for real now—spiritually speaking, "Where you at, man?" Now, you would think that that question would be rather simple to answer—but it isn't! Because ya see, biblically, there's something you need to understand: *men have a difficult time being honest!* And our difficulty being honest manifests itself in two vital matters:

1. Where we are.
2. How we got there.

And it might help you to know that we got our problem with dishonesty in those two matters—very honestly! Ya see, it was passed down to us from our great, great, great, great (you get the idea!) grandfather Adam! And in light of that, we might do well to try to glean some things from what the Scripture reveals about him from Genesis 1–3. First of all, let's talk for a second about Adam's Bible. Check this out, his entire Bible consisted of only two commands, covering a span of a whopping three verses! I mean, c'mon, man, how hard could this be, right? One of the commands had to do with Adam's relationship with his wife and the other had to do with Adam's relationship with God. The one that had to do with his wife is Genesis 1:28, where God tells him to "Be fruitful, and multiply, and replenish the earth." And I don't wanna sound crass, edgy, or off-color, but basically, what God was commanding Adam to do was to have lots of sex with the most beautiful woman in the world! And again I say, c'mon, man, how difficult could that possibly be? The other command—the one that had to do with his relationship with God, is Genesis 2:16–17, where God said, "Of every tree of the garden thou shalt freely eat: But of the tree of the knowledge of good and evil, thou shalt not eat of it: for in the day that thou eatest thereof thou shalt surely die." (KJV) And somehow in our humanness we have the ability to hear those verses and view it as a negative command about the "one tree Adam couldn't eat from" rather than hearing God saying, "Eat freely from every other tree in the garden!" But with only two commands to obey, somehow Adam found a way to blow it! And I think we're all pretty well aware of how the whole thing shook out, but let me take just a second to remind all of us of how the Scripture puts it.

Genesis 3:6–9 says, "And when the woman saw that the tree was good for food, and that it was pleasant to the eyes, and a tree to be desired to make one wise, she took of the fruit thereof, and did eat, and gave also unto her husband with her; and he did eat. And the eyes of them both were opened, and they knew that they were naked; and they sewed fig leaves together, and made themselves aprons. And they heard the voice of the Lord God walking in the garden in the cool of the day: and Adam and his wife hid themselves from the presence of the Lord God amongst the trees of the garden. And the Lord God called unto Adam, and said unto him, Where art thou?" (KJV)

And now, with that backdrop, let me share with you two principles that we desperately need to learn about ourselves that were the result of Adam's sin.

1. We are *hiders*. That is, we would rather hide than admit where we are. As we saw in Genesis 3:7–8, God comes down in the garden after man sinned, just like he had on each previous day, and in verse 9, God says, "Adam, where are you?" Now, is there any of us that thinks God didn't know exactly where Adam was? Obviously, he did. He's God, and is not only omnipresent, but omniscient! No, God asks Adam where he was to give him the opportunity to admit where he was and confess his sin! I've often wondered what the course of history would have looked like if when God called out to Adam, he would have responded with:

    "Lord, I've sinned!"
    "Father, I did the very thing you told me *not* to do!"
    "Oh, God, I've separated myself from You!"
    "Father, I chose *my way* rather than *yours*!"
    "Please forgive me!"

    But rather than coming clean with God about where he was, ya know what he does? He goes into hiding, for crying out loud! Verse 7 says he sewed fig leaves together to try to mask his problem. Oh, buddy, I bet God will never be able to see through that! And you know what the crazy thing is? Here we are, 6,000 years later, and most men find themselves exactly where Adam found himself that fateful day in the Garden! They're away from God and trying to use "fig leaves" to mask their problem. Oh, not literal fig leaves like Adam used. I'm talking about the fig leaf of their job, their career, their position, and their schedule. Or the fig leaf of their possessions (the three Cs—cars, clothes, cribs), or their bank account and financial portfolio. Or the fig leaf of any number of things: their wife, their kids, their personality, their wit, their humor, their introvertness/extrovertedness, their demeanor, their persona, their hobby, drugs, alcohol, the Internet, and on and on and on! There's a thousand different things we try to hide behind! And ya know what time it is? It's time to *man up*! It's time to stop acting like a bunch of little kids! It's time to stop acting like our problem is gonna go away if we can just hide it from everybody else!

So again, I ask you, "Where you at, man?" Do you have it in you to actually get honest with God, yourself, and the people around you—remove the fig leaves and come out from hiding? Yeah, I know—it's hard! Beastly hard! But man, is it ever freeing! But not only are men hiders who would rather hide than admit where we are.

2. We are *blame-shifters*. That is, we will shift the blame, so we don't have to admit how we got to where we are! Notice Adam's response to God's question about whether he had eaten from the forbidden tree in verse 12: "And the man said, the woman whom thou gavest to be with me, she gave me of the tree, and I did eat." (KJV) And what's really interesting is that when you first read it, it sounds like he's blaming the woman: "The woman...she gave me of the tree, and I did eat." But examine the verse closer. Look at what he actually says to God: "The woman whom thou gavest to be with me, she gave me of the tree, and I did eat." Do you hear that? He's actually blaming God for doing what he did! And I want you to know—not much has changed in the last 6,000 years! Man still has an incredible propensity to hide, and when God calls him out, rather than owning his junk, he rationalizes his guilt by shifting the blame to someone other than himself! And if

you listen long enough and are discerning enough, you'll find that who he is ultimately blaming is God! And again I say, ya know what time it is? It's time to man up! It's time, once and for all, to overcome our Adamic tendencies and propensities, come out of hiding, stop the *blame-shifting*, and become the men of God he's called us to be! We talked earlier about how different the course of history might have been if Adam would have just come clean with God. Recognize that today is your chance to change the course of history for your own life.

What Do You See in the Mirror?
by Coach Rock

Insecure as you think of Judgment Day? Lacking confidence? Living your life without a sense of destiny? Looking for that Christ-confidence that allows you to be used in a great way for the kingdom? May I put it in coaching vernacular: stop sitting on the bench and go get in the game! Here are some simple steps to get you in the end zone. Christ-confidence comes from having an eternal perspective (not trapped in the immediate). Rom. 8:28 and Phil. 1:6, bam! Nothing can keep you from God's destiny except you! It is a choice.

Living by God's promises (2 Peter 1:4) God's Word will

- Guide us with wisdom (Ps.119:105)
- Comfort us with understanding (Ps. 119:52)
- Strengthen us with boldness (Rom. 8:37)

No pun intended, but standing on the promises of God creates a firm foundation!

Trusting in our relationship with Jesus (1 John 4:4–5, Jer. 17:7) The result of such a relationship?

- You'll live up to a new level
- You'll train up in the Word
- You'll think up of your destiny

Seems everything hinges on *trust and obey*. Yea, but so often as soon as the enemy strikes, we turn and run! We have good intentions, but our actions betray our confidence. Listen, get this: those who rise above their circumstances understand that God uses every experience for good (Rom. 8:28). You are always in God's hand. Focusing (eternal perspective) upon his sovereign will and the good he has in store for you is not easy in hard times (ah, trust me on that one). I understand! But I also know that God never allows anything to touch us that he will not turn to our benefit and the good of his kingdom. So grab your helmet and get in the game!

Tackle something big for God today! I will too.

Oh, the Webb We Weave
by Coach Rock

I'm a little frustrated this morning with myself. After my devotional yesterday, I realized I had allowed my illnesses to slow me down more than I had realized. Simultaneously, I was praying in the early hours as I always do, and the Holy Spirit brought something I had read recently (from Mark Tidwell's book) to my mind. It is the story of William Webb, founder of the school that bears his name: the Webb School (located in east Tennessee).

He was raised dirt poor. His father died when he was only seven. He lived off the land with his mother and eleven siblings. He managed to gain a good education within his own home as his teacher was his sister Susan. He later in life remembered her as "the greatest teacher he ever knew." He fought in the Civil War, and when the war ended, he returned home a wounded

Confederate officer. He saw the devastation of the region and decided to start a school as he believed education to be a key to building a strong South.

Webb was a master educator. In fact, the Webb School was considered by most to be the top private school in the nation. Even to this day, Webb stands alone among the nation's elite educational institutions.

The Webb School taught governors of numerous states, a US senator, numerous Rhodes scholars, a chairman of the Federal Trade Commission, a president of the Red Cross, a US attorney general, several congressman, numerous heads of colleges, a Pulitzer Prize and Presidential Medal of Freedom winner, an editor of the *Wall Street Journal*, a *Time* magazine editor, a president of the American Bar Association, numerous physicians, lawyers, entrepreneurs, top executives of corporations, and bankers. Oh yes, one president of the United States of America, Woodrow Wilson.

But here is what I want us to focus on this day, as is always the case, anything great had great obstacles. Mr. Webb persevered through rampant disease at the school, near bankruptcy (both personal and institutional), death threats, physical attacks from locals, family tragedy and turmoil, and dire physical illness. Through it all, he remained true to his purpose and continued to teach for six decades.

On his deathbed, he dictated these thoughts to his son: "If the world is better because of you, you are a wonderful success. When you come to the end, you will find that the only things worthwhile are character and the help you've given to other people. The most important step is loyalty and obedience to God. And don't forget, don't do anything that you've got to hide."

What is it that stands between you and doing something so great it shakes the world? God says you can literally move mountains. How come we don't? I'll tell you why: we're either comfortable where we are or we've slowly allowed our life decisions to be influenced by excuses and self-doubt. Keep reading, y'all.

- "Be strong and take heart and wait for the Lord" (Ps. 27:14, NIV).
- "Blessed is the man who perseveres under trail, because when he has stood the test, he will receive the crown of life that God has promised to those who love Him" (James 1:12, NIV).
- "Let nothing move you. Always give yourselves fully to the work of the Lord, because you know that your labor is not in vain in the Lord" (1 Cor. 15:58, NIV).
- "Have faith in God, Jesus answered. I tell you the truth, if anyone says to the mountain, 'Go, throw yourself into the sea,' and does not doubt in his heart but believes that what he says will happen, it will be done for him" (Mark 11:22–23, NIV).
- "If you have faith as small as a mustard seed, you can say to this mulberry tree, 'Be uprooted and planted by the sea,' and it will obey you" (Luke 17:6, NIV).
- "Be on your guard; stand firm in the faith; be men of courage; be strong" (1 Cor 16:13, NIV).
- "I tell you the truth, anyone who has faith in Me will do what I have been doing. He will do even greater things than these, because I am going to the Father" (John 14:12, NIV).

My Father is with me wherever I go. He will never leave me or forsake me. He tells me to be strong and courageous, not comfortable or playing it safe. As he told Isaiah (who jumped to his feet and said "Here am I send me!"), "So do no fear, for I am with you; do not be dismayed, for I am your God. I will strengthen you and help you; I will uphold you with My righteous right hand." Paul shouted loud enough we here the echo today, "I can do everything through Him who gives me strength."

4.5 billion souls need our love, our message, our Jesus. I will break every stronghold and I will move that mountain. I'm shooting for the impossible! You too?

GRIDIRON GOSSIP AND GRAFFITI

B onus material might be the best way to describe this chapter. I'm just going to ramble on about some facts, figures, and the folklore I'm sure will make for an interesting read, especially for those former players, parents, boosters, church friends, fellow coaching buddies, family. It will be quite random in terms of chronology. As it comes to me, it will come to you. Let's get started, shall we?

Did you know I was the head coach of an Arena II team (indoor professional football)? I did it during one off-season (December to February). I got paid about 1/3 of what I signed on for, so I quit with about a month to go. It was not a good experience. If I remember right, I took over a team that was several games under .500, and during my tenure, we went 5-4. The highlight of the experience was getting to know our rivals head coach John Fourcade. John was the "scab" QB for the Saints during the strike year of the NFL. He was an Ole Miss legend and quite the character. I beat him both times we played, and we developed a close relationship. The worst part of that season was the death of one of our players. The most delightful player on the roster was a former star cornerback for LSU, Chris Beard. He was such a friendly, polite, and articulate kid. I admit, he was my favorite. In fact, we liked him so much we hired to be a full-time corporate sales executive for us. However, during a game late in the season, he made a tackle and never got up. He suffered total paralysis and died from a freak accident. Beard, thereafter confined to a wheelchair, later died when a pet dog jumped on his lap, cutting off Beard's air supply. Chris was just twenty-four years old. I think of him to this day quite often.

Did you know I made an All-Knapp thirty-year team? Yes, I did. However, I keep it under heavy security and have not even shared it with my sons. Obviously, if I share it publicly, there will be some very disappointed grown men and certain hurt feelings. Well, suck it up, gentlemen, these are my opinions. Yours may differ and yours may be more accurate than mine. If you do disagree, please don't hesitate to send me your perspective. It should make for good debate between you and me as well as you and your teammates. So here we go.

All Knapp All-Americans

All Knapp Wide Outs: Hank Lankford (Newnan Christian), John Brooks (Westminster), Teddy Knapp, (Riverdale Baptist), Craig Cieslik (Antelope Valley Christian)

All Knapp Backfield: Chris Edwards (Westminster), Nile Knapp (Southwest Georgia Academy), Reid McMilion (Morgan Academy), Honorable Mention: Craig Lewis (Riverdale Baptist)

All Knapp Triggerman: Mike Kershaw (Westminster), John Tharp (Houston Christian), Kris Kershaw (Antelope Valley Christian), Honorable Mention: Tim Pullin (Landmark)

All Knapp Tight End: Joel Comeaux (Westminster), Eric Harrison (Riverdale Baptist)

All Knapp Offensive line: Diego London (Riverdale Baptist), Jason Burns (Riverdale Baptist), Shelton Jordan (Westminster), Alfie Schaeffer (Middletown Christian), Andrew Lowman

(Riverdale Baptist), Jimmy Dean (Riverdale Baptist), Hobie White (Landmark), Khalid Kahlef (Houston Christian), Greg Parrish, (Temple Heights Christian School)
All Knapp Center: Tony Radcliffe (Houston Christian), Kevin Lee (Antelope Valley Christian), Seth Benhard (Westminster)
All Knapp Special Team: Kickers: Alex Scheuermann (Westminster), Troy Harvell (Morgan Academy), Rick Stevens (Riverdale Baptist), Honorable Mention: Donnie Carroll (Houston Christian)
All Knapp Special Team Player: Reggie Richard (Westminster), Trent Claxon (Middletown Christian)
All Knapp Athlete (most versatile): Donnie Adams (Landmark), Nate Harvey (Riverdale Baptist)
All Knapp Most Improved (from one year to the next): Jeremy Edwards (Westminster), Ellis Dupre (Westminster), Alex Rodriguez (Summit Christian), Ray Jones III (Summit Christian)
All Knapp Christian Character Award: Mark Tidwell (Newnan Christian), Chris Abernathy (Northwest Academy), Andrew Consolver (Canyon Creek Christian), Jonathan Wheeler (Middletown Christian)
All Knapp Defensive Line: Jason Burns (Riverdale Baptist), Mike Batenga (Riverdale Baptist), Diego London (Riverdale Baptist)
All Knapp Defensive End: David Turner (Houston Christian), Adam Jacobs (Houston Christian), Michael Lovelady (Houston Christian)
All Knapp Linebacker: Curtis Jackson (Houston Christian), Mike Connell (Houston Christian), Reggie Nelams (Westminster)
All Knapp Secondary: Scott Toregrossa (Riverdale Baptist), David Bradford (Morgan Academy), Trent Claxon (Middletown Christian), Josh Trantham (Houston Christian), Brandon White (Houston Christian)
All Knapp Hardest Worker Every day: Brooks Bellow (Westminster)

All Knapp Scariest Player in Uniform: 2,500 players through three decades and I had some very good looking football players who looked like they belonged in the NFL. However, no one looked as daunting as David Turner.

U150 Team: Greg Fort (Riverdale), Alex Rodriguez (Summit Christian), Vinny Galis (Antelope Valley Christian), Beau Marks (Westminster), Brooks Bellow (Westminster), Andrew Neidhammer (Riverdale Baptist), Reggie Richard (Westminster), Carl Dimuzio (Riverdale Baptist)

Most Valued: Each night for thirty years, I would end up sitting down to supper only to find my whistle in my spaghetti or macaroni as it hung around my neck. It always brought a smile to my face. You see, that whistle was a part of me, the coach. And every player in whose direction I blew that whistle is forever a part of me. And so it is, I will be buried with my whistle around my neck and I'll be looking forward to glory and playing catch with Jimbo, Danny, Brooks, Joey, and Mark...no whistle needed!

Many have asked about who was the best team? Rank my top ten. Talk about wishy-washy. I vacillate between four teams that I honestly do not know who would be the top, but you paid for an opinion, not a copout, so here ya go, boys:

1. Riverdale Baptist (year 2)
2. Morgan Academy (1985)
3. Houston Christian (lost state title in overtime)
4. Westminster (year 2)

Biggest team? Riverdale Baptist my second year, we were mammoth. I mean across the front 7, we were a solid 280 lbs. Diego London, who signed with the Miami Hurricanes (and won three national titles while there), was 6'5" and 320 lbs. We really were as big as a lot of college teams. Fastest team? I'd have to go with Morgan Academy out of Selma, Alabama. Spent just one year there, went 10-2 and played for the state title. I had legit six players on the field at any one time that could run the 100m in 10 something. My quarterback who went to West Point to play was actually named Clayton Speed! A close second would have to be my last squad at Houston Christian, my quarterback not withstanding…LOL. Poor John, a football IQ off the charts, a savvy arm, solid leader, and maybe the slowest human to ever wear a helmet. Otherwise, we had some very fast people. My favorite team, keep in mind (and this is not just coach's speak here) I have such a love and fondness for each team I coached. However, I suppose if I had to pick, it would be my Westminster team of year two. The Cajun people are an irresistible culture. If they love you—man, they love you! My friendships, support, and our incredible run just made the magic so over-the-top I'd have to give them the nod. MVP of thirty years? I'm actually going to tell you that one. There are so many just a hair behind this guy I've picked. I mean I had about a dozen guys who are right there: Curtis at Linebacker, Chris at RB, Nile at RB, Hank at WR, Diego at OL, Jason at DL, Reid at FB, on and on it goes including the incredible deep snapping of Joel Comeaux, good enough to sign a full scholarship to play 1AA at receiver/TE but was by far the most prolific deep snapper I have ever seen. Yes, better than *any* deep snapper in the NFL, period. Anyway, the best player I ever coached: Mike Kershaw. Here's why. Mike was the smartest player I ever coached. He had an understanding of the game that was uncanny. His instincts were always right. He was so poised under pressure—nothing rattled him. His arm was a rocket and his accuracy so on-the-spot. Mike never made a mistake…just didn't. Led us to a nice two-year undefeated run. I pick him because he did the most good things of my three decades of players. Kris and John were both right there too. But then I think about guys like Tim Pullin who played QB and without a lot of skill, but with a lot of heart found a way to lead his team to an undefeated season in '84. Guys like that make me smile and what an honor to be their coach. Which team was the deepest in the pooper when I got there? Probably Northwest Academy (Houston Christian). They were 0-39 the last four years and the weight room/locker room were atrocious. We were 6-4 the first season followed by three straight appearances in the state championship. Sherwood would be a close second, I guess (so would Antelope Valley). Sherwood had gone twenty-three seasons without a winning record. Antelope Valley was all but folded when I took the reigns, 13-0 state champs! Best headmaster? Tie between Dr. Billings and Dr. Holzman. My favorite football coach was Knute Rockne, Hayden Fry would be a close second, and finishing in the money would be Rock Royer…look his bio up sometime. Picture I wish I had that I don't: the Four Horsemen of Notre Dame. Favorite uniforms: year 2 at Riverdale and year 2 at Westminster. I had two handicapped players who had no business playing football make it through the whole season: Mike White who played with one leg completely disfigured (Riverdale)—he did not get much playing time however, but his courage and want to were a fine example for all. Chris Cundiff played wide receiver and DB for us in Middletown Ohio. He has one arm and hand that were deformed. He was a fine receiver and he was fun to watch on a basketball court. In spite of just one workable arm, Chris was a standout athlete. My one tie (a 36-36 shootout) was when I was at Middletown Christian (Ohio) against Hammond Baptist who came into the game at 9-0. We were 7-2. The temperature that night was in the 20s. Best opposing player…can't remember the kid's name and he did not go on to play D1 either as I remember. But for two years, the kid was a monster on the field and just ate our lunch. He was a Hispanic kid from St. Pius, played fullback and linebacker. I loved how he played the game. Total reckless abandonment, full tilt every play. And he played like he wanted to kill somebody. My two favorite opposing coaches were Chuck

Faucette of Pius in Houston and Mike Hall of Second Baptist in Houston. Never lost to Chuck, never beat Mike.

The toughest loss was the 77-20 beat down we took from Mike Hall and his Second Baptist Eagles. Humiliating to say the least. I hurt really bad for our kids. A close second would be our play-off loss to Sarasota Booker (7-6) while at Temple Heights in Tampa. They went on to win the state title. We were so close to the upset of the year in Florida. We dropped a 2-point conversion pass that would have won it. And finishing third in our heartbreak category would be our overtime loss in the Texas 4A state title game (21-14) to Dallas Christian. With four seconds left in regulation, we attempted a 16-yard field goal for the win. Our all-state kicker who had not missed one all year was a foot wide right as time expired.

Injuries? In thirty years, I had but one serious injury, and it ended happily ever after. Brandon Scardino, a linebacker at Canyon Creek (and a good one!), stepped into an off-tackle play to take on a running back and the opponent rammed his helmet right into Brandon's solar plexus and it immediately ruptured his spleen. Within the hour of the injury, he was in surgery. By 4:00 a.m., we were sitting bedside talking about the game.

What I would change if I could go back in time and do it all over again? Less yelling. Secondly, I'd have learned to keep my mouth shut when I had differences of opinions with a sorry headmaster. Just focus on the kids and work within the parameters I had been given.

My favorite manager of all time? No contest, Robert Ring at Houston Christian. Robert was so good we gave him keys to everything. He went on to college as a football manager. He was so committed, hardworking, trustworthy, and loyal. I loved that guy!

Our best cheerleading sponsor and squad? Kathy Todoroff and the ladies of Northwest/HCHS. They spoiled us, man, oh, man, did they spoil us. And they were very, very good, brought home a lot of hardware from summer competitions.

Best week of football ever? Gulf South Football Camp, Opelousas, Louisiana. I hosted a week-long overnight football camp while at Westminster Christian Academy. It was a riot! I had numerous ex-pro's (including Super Bowl MVP Doug Williams) and college and NFL coaches on staff, former players who had gone on to play in the NFL/CFL come and be counselors and instructors. We spent time every day at Little Teche Farms utilizing their pool, lodge, grills, food, the list goes on. We had several hundred campers making us the largest overnight camp west of the Mississippi. It was a perfect week, and I have never laughed that hard again.

Best scouts? Easy, Billy and Eddie, Northwest Academy. Those to cats were all business and gave us an edge going into each week of preparation. Not to mention, two of the best men on the planet.

Best announcer ever: Larry Orlando at Houston Christian.

Here is something you may not know. The private schools in Texas have kick started the all-star football game again. I started the event with the Bayou Bowl. It was for seniors to showcase their talent and give one last opportunity to earn a scholarship to the next level. The game was renamed the Lone Star Christian Sports Network Ted "Rock" Knapp All-Star Football Classic. I have been very honored by such a gesture. I am planning on attending this years' weekend celebration and game in December, Lord willing and the creek don't rise, I'll make the "Rock Bowl!"

Anyone who knows me knows my biggest win wasn't even a game. It was a scrimmage! We made history the day we tackled Cincinnati Moeller and won by TKO. And who can forget our 29-14 win over Southern Lab or Newnan Christian coming back from 14-0 to win the state title 30-14. (Which was the only place we had a state title parade. We went through downtown Newnan with quite a good crowd to cheer us after winning it all. We were on floats and convertibles and had a steady applause and thumbs-up all the way up and down the main drag.) The two big semifinal wins at Houston Christian where we beat Midland Christian 7-6 in the last few minutes and then our sweetest revenge game over my thirty years was the 31-28 win over Liberty Christian in the semi's after suffering a 35-0 blow out loss to their same team the year before in the state title game. The day we beat them, we snapped a 27-game win streak.

Best road trip would have to be our flight and weeks' stay out in Colorado Springs for pre-season football camp. We fund-raised the entire off-season, and man, what a blast! We toured the Air Force Academy, practiced on their turf field, scrimmaged two 4A public schools, and beat them both. We stayed on a small mountain at a Southern Baptist camp facility.

My favorite postgame activity was hands down late evening meals at Tony Roma's with Phil Kershaw. Phil was wonderful conversation as we evaluated the game almost play-by-play. He was a master at making you feel like you just won the Super Bowl and were the best coach in America. Of course, Tony Roma ribs made it perfect.

There are so many memories like this one that are so special it is difficult to try and capture their magic in a single paragraph. I remember before the Ribet game (California) telling Jay Elliott (long-time assistant coach) that if we beat Ribet, a team that had incredible athletes and way more speed than us, Jay and I were going to drive his pickup out into the country, sit on the back gate, smoke a cigar (which I may have had one in my entire life), and stare at the stars and tell each other how great we were. Sure enough, we got the 40-20 win and puffed our way to greatness that night.

My mentors: Ron Black, Audie Johnson, Phil Kershaw. Without the influence of these three men, I'd have been selling insurance or used cars by 1990. Best "partner" I ever worked with:

Janie Neighbors. What a coach, what a teacher, what a friend. I love you, Janie.

My favorite booster club member over thirty years (oh my, have I had hundreds of great friends come along side and make a real difference for the boys), if I could just pick one, it would be the amazing Marla Chambless. Endless, boundless energy. What a servant's heart, love each boy like they were her own children. Her support, sacrifice of time and talent was a daily encouragement to me. I miss her and Jerry. They remain our good friends.

Player who I enjoyed watching more than all the other players through the years? Tie. And they played together. John Tharp and Mike Connell. John was a kid with about zero athletic ability for football: skinny, weak core strength, shy, maybe 5'11", 145 lbs. One day, I was just standing around before the start of practice and all the boys were on the field just playing catch when I happened to notice John. He was throwing this perfect spiral: good velocity on the ball, quick release to top it all off. I had a hunch about the kid. Man, was I right. Tharp was stellar. Best QB in 4A as far as I was concerned. And Mike Connell, he was an undersized linebacker who played with reckless abandon and a mean streak that earned him the nickname "Taz" (short for Tazmanian Devil!). Mike played like his hair was on fire. We loved turning the Taz loose on Friday nights!

Best band. Easy. The bunch from Southern Lab. Reminded me of Grambling. My favorite college band: Grambling! Best thing about college football? The LSU Golden Girls. The best college fans: Nebraska (1), Texas A&M (2) LSU (3).

In my mind, the worst game I coached in my career? It was the state title game versus Arlington Christian at Baylor. We got hammered 35-17. I was mean and irritable during the game, and our prep that week was very much skewed by my conflict with an out-of-control parent. I had to fire a coach earlier in the week, and we just never got on tract.

If I could have one wish, I'd have liked to see how good we could have been with Chris Edwards, Nile Knapp, and Reid McMilion all in the backfield together. I know this much, they would be the best backfield trio in America…period.

Best venue in thirty years: H. E. B. Stadium in Arlington, Texas. What a stadium for high school football! By a ton, the best of them all. Worst field? Easy. The cow pasture up in El Dorado, Arkansas. The rocks presented a slight challenge, so we decided not to get tackled. We won like 65-0. A close second was Balch Springs Christian in Texas. It rained unbelievably and we played in six inches of pure mud. Again, we won 56-0. Our biggest opponent that night: ants!

Best fan: George Griffin, of course. He carried our school flag along to every game. Ran up and down the sideline with that flag more than I went up and down it! One great supporter of Riverdale Baptist School for thirty years. What a dear friend. I love you, George!

Lastly, my favorite two plays. The extra point pass remains number 1. It either scored a TD or got us a critical first down always at the right moment. Second best play is a little off the beaten path. It was my Riverdale team. We decided to schedule a prep team out of Delaware (fifth year seniors). The refs had no patches, I knew we were in trouble. Anyway, during the game they made this incredibly dishonest call, and I blew my cork. I walked out to midfield, called them all a not-so-nice name, "You dudes are so ghetto." All at once, five flags all go into the air. As I walked off the field, I just started picking up their flags. I got to the sideline and walked over to the coolers, took the lid off one of them, and stuffed the flags down in the bottom of the water cooler. They tossed me from the stadium and finally realized their flags were missing. Our kids said nothing. We won 20-0. Our boys referred to it as our one and only flag football game; one of my assistant coaches brought me the flags after the game. I display them from time to time when speaking at coaches clinics.

Oh, dear reader, the stories are endless, the memories are endless, and I wish to be remembered in an endless legacy as simply "coach." Now, where did I put that whistle?

ABOUT THE AUTHOR

Coach Rock has won nine state titles in six different states as a high school football coach. In 1997–98 he was selected the Texas Private and Parochial Football Coach of the Year. He is a former sports radio talk show host, a motivational speaker, speaking at school chapels, churches, athletic banquets, and football clinics. In 2008 he was diagnosed with two terminal diseases. He has been married to the former Shari Lykins of Louisville, Kentucky for thirty-four years. Together, they have five children and nine grandchildren.